INSIDE AMATEUR
PHOTOGRAPHY

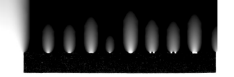

INSIDE AMATEUR
PHOTOGRAPHY

DAVE KENYON

Series Editor: John Izod, Department of Film and
Media Studies, University of Stirling

B. T. Batsford Ltd, London

© David Kenyon 1992
First published 1992

Typeset by Servis Filmsetting Ltd, Manchester
and printed in Great Britain by BPCC Hazells Ltd

Published by B. T. Batsford Ltd
4 Fitzhardinge Street, London W1H 0AH

A CIP catalogue record for this book is
available from the British Library

ISBN 0 7134 6774 6

CONTENTS

ACKNOWLEDGMENTS

I would like to thank the following bodies for their support and co-operation:

Agfa; *The Amateur Photographer*; Canon; Dartington College of Arts (especially its library staff); the Elmgrant Trust; Ilford; Leica; the National Museum Of Photography, Film And Television; The Open University; The Royal Photographic Society; The University Of Stirling Department Of Film And Media Studies.

I am also indebted to those who have commented upon drafts and offered encouragement: Roger Dennis, John Izod, Jo Spence, Steve Taylor.

Certain individuals have been kind enough to give permission for images in their possession to be reproduced here. Thanks are due to: Grace Baker, Evelyn Edwards, Richard Goldsmith and family, Colin Gordon, Ray Hopley and family, Louise Johnson, Mike and Patsy Martin, John Pullen and family, Kent Shelley, Kenny, and of course, my family.

I would also like to thank all those who have opened up their collections to me, but whose images I have not reproduced here.

Finally I am grateful to John Gridley, Steve Hoare and the students on the "Art and Social Context" course at Dartington for their continued commitment to art and people which provided a stimulating environment to nurture the ideas in this book. The course will be sorely missed.

INTRODUCTION

This book is intended to be provocative: it seeks to inform and challenge readers to think about amateur photography for themselves. We are all some sort of expert on our own experience, and most of us have experienced taking photos. What we often lack are alternative views, theories and methods which, if brought to bear on this experience, might enrich it.

The project

When people think of photography, they usually think of 'taking a picture'. The more technically minded may abstract out light's chemical action on a sensitive medium, aided by lenses. Dictionaries also stress this. *Photography*, they tell us, is rooted in two Greek terms *phot* (light) and *graphein* (to write).

This book is concerned with photography as a social act. 'Taking a picture' may be central to this act, but that's not all there is to it. The often emphasized chemical and optical nature of photography is important for its status as a recording medium, but this too must take its place as only one of several elements.

What is deemed photographable and why? What are the pictures of? How do we come by them? Who takes the photos? What do we think we're doing when we take them?

Then again, what *don't* we do when we're photographing and what do we do with our photos when we've got them? These are some of the questions that become central when we take up the study of everyday photography as popular culture.

Why might it be useful or interesting to study our photography in this way? Well, it is one of the few areas which bridges our public and private worlds. Snaps share with private diaries the potential to make our everyday assumptions, our hopes and fears, accessible to others. (And snaps are much easier to see than diaries.) They document the private pleasures and rituals of everyday life, and can make them available to a wider audience. This photography can also tell us something about our relationships with our nearest and dearest, because these are the people it is initially aimed at. Through the medium of the family photo collection, we can all grow to understand the rules and norms of domestic existence a little better.

Despite its role in everyday experience, amateur photography is not central to any of society's major institutions, nor is it the subject of public resourcing. Because of this it hardly gets considered by the constant flow of social commentary related to education, communication, the law, religion or government. Yet its intimate connection to our experience can throw light on the ways such institutions affect us.

In such social research, the case study, in-depth interview, and participant observer approaches can produce detailed and convincing human data. But with in-depth techniques, the question often remains: are the cases, interviewees, or social groups studied representative? Using snaps as the material through which we consider the social act of domestic photography helps with the problem of representativeness. The context of other people's photographic efforts enables us to build up a picture of how representative a person's photos and experience are. We can compare someone's shots with those of others and categorize them on the basis of shared attributes. At the same time, the depth of understanding available via the individual photographs and associated experience is not lost. It appears that we can 'have our cake and eat it'. If this is true, it makes the study of amateur photography all the more productive.

Words: much more than 1/1000th of a picture

This book's approach is allied to that of cultural studies which is an interdisciplinary field. One of its foundation stones is the study of literature and literary theory. Consequently, it is commonplace for the approach to begin by concerning itself with the history of the changing uses of words central to the area. The excellent book *Keywords* by Raymond Williams[1] does this for some central terms in the general study of English speaking culture.

In more specialized fields one can turn to dictionaries for the derivation and morphology of words. The standard English authority is the Oxford English Dictionary [O.E.D.]. In the case of our everyday photography, the words *amateur* and *professional*, currently used as antonyms, would seem a good place to start. Amateur currently connotes: naive, inadequate, unskilled, uninspiring. On the other hand, professional connotes: skilled and knowledgeable (interestingly not necessarily inspiring).

Looking up 'amateur' in the O.E.D. shows us that the word is relatively new to the English language, and between its introduction in the late eighteenth century and the early nineteenth, it simply meant someone fond of something, ('enamoured' comes from the same root). Around 1803 it began to be used to distinguish those whose interest was untainted by concerns for financial gain. By the middle 1800s the word was consistently contrasted to professional, either approvingly or disparagingly. By the 1860s it would seem that the modern meaning of the word was pretty well established. Crucial to this establishment was the history of its antonym, 'professional'.

'Professional' is a much older word in English, and its history is a telling one. Originally relating to those in a religious position who had professed their vows, in the sixteenth century it was broadened out to apply to the three 'learned professions' studied at university (Divinity, Law and Medicine). These all had some solemn oath associated with entry to them, and were only open to gentlemen (whose word was their bond). In the later sixteenth century the term began to be widened further by including other occupations – importantly those 'socially superior to a trade or handicraft' [O.E.D.].

Groups who at that time had no place in the traditional elite, were pressing to assert their rights to similar respect and similar remuneration as the learned professions enjoyed, and they sought to do this by aligning their business with the professions as against the skilled trades.

This procedure, whereby an increasing number of occupations gain access to professional status, continues up to the present day. But it reached its zenith in the Victorian era. At this time there were, on the one hand, the upper-class gentlemen amateurs who questioned the integrity of the aspiring middle-class 'professionals'. On the other, there were the new professionals themselves, who were keen to press their case for social recognition and economic reward. In part, their challenge took the form of trying to undermine the position of the upper-class amateur by asserting lack of experience and dilettantism as concommitant properties of amateurism. It is a matter of historical fact who gained the upper hand politically in the nineteenth century, but we still live with the words as constructed then, that is, with 'professional' having far higher status. So the histories of the words *professional* and *amateur* are intertwined with those of class development.

It is important to point out that underlying this quick review of word usage is an assumption that the words we use are not transparent labels for the 'real' world. Not only do they carry with them the marks of political and economic struggle, they are also weapons in those struggles. When we use them we enter into a politics which is not of our making, but which we can never avoid.

When the word 'amateur' is used in this book it is intended to carry these connotions: *naive* – in the sense of being less predicated on commercial concerns and the notions of 'correctness' that follow in professional practice. *Popular* – in the sense that it is enjoyed by a majority. *Everyday* – in as much as it is always happening somewhere at any one time. *Domestic* – to the extent that one's household and family are the catalyst to the activity.

It is not intended to mobilize the negative connotations of inadequacy, lack-of-skill, ephemerality etc. which dog the word. However, because of these connotations, the word *vernacular* has often been used as a synonym for the positive side of amateur throughout the text. Vernacular photography is the shared picture language of ordinary people.

This book attempts to champion a new respect for the importance of 'amateur culture', as instanced not only by vernacular photography, but also by gardening, DIY, knitting and every other leisure pursuit which combines creative expression and social experience. As such it seeks to re-engage in the battle for meaning won by the middle-class professionals of the past, and to reassert the value of the amateur. And this time almost everyone in 'the photographing nations' can afford the entry price.

A history of popular photography

Although based upon principles of optics known for centuries, apparatus familiar since the late Renaissance and chemical properties discovered early in the eighteenth century, photography is a child of the nineteenth century. It was the intellectual, social and economic outlook of the industrial revolution that really got it going. Early photographic experiments tried to mechanize drawing and thereby to use science to aid faltering humanity's efforts to record people and places – a project very much in tune with the prevailing attitudes. At the same time these experiments attempted to gain commercial advantage by reducing the labour involved in the printing industry.

The first experimenters were mainly gentlemen scientists, with incomes guaranteed by who they were, rather than by what they did. An exception was Daguerre,[1] a successful French cultural entrepreneur. Before he became associated with photography he produced life-size dioramas, specializing in optical effects. In short, he was an upmarket showman.

Professionals

Daguerre and his process led to the development of the photographer's trade. Generally, this was only open to those members of the upper classes who could raise the necessary capital. However, many of those who did have access to some capital could not look forward to sufficient income from its investment alone. They needed a lucrative profession. So they took up photography, a trade with potentially dazzling returns.

Initially, professional photography was largely synonymous with portraiture. This was almost wholly carried on by daguerreotypists because of the superior detail of this technique compared to the alternative paper processes. Daguerreotype was an extremely lucrative business. The results it produced were at once delicate and precious. They necessitated careful framing and resulted in an object comparable in status to the much more expensive painted miniature.

In the 1840s, photographers such as R. Beard in London could make twenty times a working man's yearly wage in one month![2] However, such extraordinary profitability created its own industry of litigations. The rules of ownership and rights to exploitation were still being fought over. The photographic image was not only immensely profitable, it was also a challenge to the notions of creative rights.[3] Because of this, patent and copyright lawsuits have characterised photography since its beginnings. William Fox Talbot, the English inventor of the paper negative process, attempted to protect it and endured loss of esteem and money in the course of the legal battles. Beard, probably professional photography's first millionaire, prosecuted several people he considered to have infringed his patents. The result was profit for the lawyers, but bankruptcy for Beard.

The stakes have always been high, and as long as photography continues to be a growth industry the number of litigations will not diminish. The Kodak v Polaroid debacle of the 1970–80s is only the most publicized recent example [see p. 94].

Amateurs

Professional photography has always had a complex symbiotic relationship with amateur photography. The profession is constantly revitalized by amateurs, and amateurs are endlessly stimulated by professional work.

For the first thirty years of photography, most amateur's first encounter was via the High Street portraitists. (Indeed, it is only very recently, that they have been displaced from their role as 'photographer by appointment' to the casual amateur, as opposed to the 'serious amateur' [see p. 54–5]). It was this early vogue for the studio likeness which first gave historians a picture of a whole strata of society – the middle classes.

Starting from largely aristocratic beginnings, amateur photography filtered slowly down through income brackets and social classes, only reaching the large majority in Europe in the 1950s. From its beginning it was associated with tourism and holidays away from home. Initially it was only industrialists and the gentry who had such leisure pursuits. But as the capitalist states began to need to buy stability through reforms to the basic wage labour system, the introduction of statutory holidays, and later, paid holidays, increased the opportunities for people to have specified leisure periods.[4] These 'time outs' were worth recording in some fashion, if only by virtue of their difference to the everyday.

The Western economies were growing; and from the mid 1870s onwards management, clerical and skilled technical jobs proliferated. With this came an increase in the number of people in the lower-middle income brackets. By the 1890s, the new middle classes followed those who previously, by virtue of their success as capitalists, had achieved the leisure and disposable income to take up photography. The lower-middle classes (clerks, lower management

Carte de visite: From the 1860s to the late 1880s, small photos like this constituted most people's experience of photographs. The size continued to be popular up to the First World War, but usually for vignetted portraits. These four from different towns in Scotland and England illustrate the highly formulaic nature of their representations.

Cabinet photographs: These larger pictures displaced the cartes in the late 1880s as the format for full-length and family group photos. They were less formulaic, and by the end of the century may have been taken outdoors.

Holidays: (Torbay Sands circa 1914). Southern resorts show a general tendancy to be developed for London's small capitalists' families, and then to be taken over gradually by the less well-to-do. As this happened, those who could afford it moved further afield.

etc.) and the skilled artisan, still didn't have the spare cash to take it up themselves, and on their day-trips and infrequent holidays they used the professionals' services to furnish them with their mementos. Then, in the 1900s when paid holidays were introduced, even the working classes could buy this surrogate 'amateur' photography.

For all classes photography was only one of a number of competing outlets for the expenditure of surplus income. Many of these

were much more functional than photography and normally sup-
planted it. After the rent (or mortgage) and servants had been paid,
and the family fed, there was the cost of travel to those events which
it might have been nice to record (if the money hadn't been spent
getting there!). A bicycle, and later a car, might call upon the money
first because they could be used for work, not just leisure. Domestic
appliances, such as the sewing machine, could produce savings or
even income, and so would probably have come before cameras in
the houshold's priorities.

Families with a lot of children had very little spare cash; indeed, it
was the voluntary lowering of the birth rate which made most
difference to standards of living for everyone throughout the
modern period.[5] Because men's wages were roughly double
women's and single men could avoid the financial burden of family
responsibilities, the latter were most likely to take up photography
as the overall conditions of their class improved. Often these young
men would act as the group photographer for a peer group; documenting the shared experience of holiday, cycle tour, coach trip or
car ride etc. In this way the others in the group got their mementos
without needing to take up photography themselves. It was only in
the late 1930s that the Western economies really began to address
the problem of poverty that was seriously affecting almost a third of
the population.[6] Before then, this large section of society had no

**Charabanc Trip: Prior to World War Two, certain young men would become the
'amateur' community photographer by virtue of recording the events they were
involved in. Many people's photos came from such friends, rather than the studio
cartes of the previous century.**

spare cash to put into anything as unproductive as photography. The poor may have had a one-off High Street photographer's studio portrait, or possibly in a good year, the day-trip's tintype from an itinerant photographer, but owning a camera – even a brownie (and in additon paying for developing and printing) was out of the question. George Eastman and his Kodak are often cited as the beginnings of mass popular photography in 1888.[7] This is not so; with the Kodak and the brownie especially, amateur photography was taken to a sizeable proportion of the lower-middle classes, but not to the working class.

Exceptions to these general rules were those single males who, by virtue of skilled labour, or membership of the armed forces (an early area of high photographic take-up) had the combination of spare cash, lack of financial responsibilities and few competing outlets for their leisure expenditure.

Technological additions resulting in the increased flexibility of the process are generally seen as the stimuli for the diffusion of photography throughout our modern culture. However, large changes in economic distribution and employment conditions were much more important. The profitability and resultant competitiveness of the photographic industry forced enterprises to be inventive. The end of workshop manufacture and the introduction of assembly-line working (made famous by Henry Ford and widespread by the time of the First World War), lowered unit costs and increased sales. Most importantly, the expansion of the service sector and the concomitant rise in the professional and lower-middle classes, coupled with their increasing spare cash, created potential consumers on a scale previously unknown.

Beginning in the 1930s, cigarette firms offered cameras and films for coupons. This spread the ownership of cameras and resulted in many household members combining their coupons to buy 'family' cameras. However, printing a film's pictures cost an hour and a half's wages.[8] Although consumer credit appeared during this period, few people who needed it for cameras could get it. As is still the case, credit is available to people who have some money, to encourage them to spend more. So credit was used by the middle classes to buy cameras like the new Leica, (which, at £18. 15., was worth over six week's wages for most workers of the time).[9]

During the 1930s a movement arose, most prevalent in Germany, in which workers, for so long merely the possessors of cheap professional photographs, clubbed together to own cameras and process their results. This was an overtly political project and aimed to record workers' lives from their own point of view. These images were then used in their own radical publications. In this way they

"Seen these daddy -

Dick's just developed them — he says they're perfect—even though I took some of them ; he says it's 'cos Kodak films are always made to allow a wide margin of error. I don't know what he means, but, anyway, he told me to ask you to get him some more; he knows you won't take long 'cos he says he knows you're a whale for ' Black Cats.' "

For 40 coupons from Black Cat Cigarettes you can have a Kodak Film No. 120 — takes pictures $3\frac{1}{4}'' \times 2\frac{1}{4}''$—Obtainable Everywhere

Kodak
ROLL FILM
free FOR 40
COUPONS

Kodak Film

---

5 FREE COUPONS

(Dept. KM), Gifts Dept.,
CARRERAS LTD.,
Arcadia Works, Hampstead Road,
London, N.W.1

Please send me Free Booklet and Five Free Coupons.

Name ....

Address ....

....

Only One of these signed Coupons accepted.

Black Cat
VIRGINIA CIGARETTES
10 for 6ᵈ   20 for 1⁴

Only a good gift with a good name is good enough for a good cigarette.

Cigarettes and photos: These offers are advertised using the now familiar techniques of showing children and women as able to cope with photography – and desiring the expenditure.

hoped to achieve control over their political visibility.[10] The approach has been influential in recent radical photographic practice. So-called 'minority' groups are attempting to make their experiences public, and thereby place them on the political agenda, through photography and other media.[11]

After the Second World War, photography really became cheap enough for almost everyone in the Western economies. Workers' standards of living at last allowed this sort of leisure expenditure. Production line mechanization introduced from Japan made the hardware relatively cheap, and mechanized processing dropped the costs of getting results. The washing machine and other useful appliances took precedence in household expenditure. However, as before with the other income groups, the single male would bring the camera into the household sooner or later.

Women and early photography

So, if amateur photography for the bottom half of society was largely a practice for the single male, what of women's involvement?

At first sight, women don't seem to figure in the earliest days of photography. But this is a result of the general invisibility of women in male dominated cultures. Constance, Talbot's wife, helped him in his experiments, although he seldom mentioned this. Daguerre's optical supplier, Giroux, used his wife's daguerreotypes to advertise his cameras. The 'invisible helpmate' was relatively common. Some gentlemen amateurs who claimed authorship of images actually used their spouses or menservants, to take – and process – the images.

In the early days, women were more involved in the professional practice than the amateur. The economics of starting small businesses resulted in unsung husband/wife 'partnerships' as much then as today. The noxious fumes involved in the early processes frequently caused disability, or even fatality. Photographers' wives often kept the businesses going when their husbands no longer could. They seldom had any other choice.

This early involvement with professional photography opened up the trade to women at a time when respectable occupations for middle-class women were thought particularly necessary due to the smaller number of eligible men at this time. As a potentially lucrative profession, it was more secure than some others, (a career on the stage for example).[12] It was also more accessible than other professions which still operated bars to women, or at least, strong discouragement. Hull in north-east England can claim the first recorded woman professional photographer, a Mrs Cooke. She set up shop in 1842, only three years after the publication of the photographic process.

However, the vast majority of women involved in photography were employed as 'unskilled' process workers due to their availability and low pay. It is not recorded how many of them suffered illness, even death, as a result of the chemicals involved. For them it was possibly a job on a par with the sweatshops of the garment trade, or perhaps a little better. Some women lived in as housekeepers and worked in the business as well, echoing the position of thousands of female domestic servants at the time.

Another significant group of women workers in the photographic industry were 'artist's models'. The female nude was, in 1841, almost the first human image to be offered for sale as a photograph. These images provided vicarious sexual enjoyment for a frustrated male middle class who practised sexual abstinence at home, largely in order to balance the domestic budget. They could not afford to live up to their position in life, *and* pay for large families. So, in the absence of effective or ethically sanctioned birth control, these men took their enjoyment outside the family.[13]

In some senses the role of photographic model is a success story for women's employment. Although only open to women who conform to the commercially exploitable notions of attractiveness, the field of modelling has exploded in terms of size, opportunity and lucrativeness. Women are required to adorn images of everything

Women process workers (circa 1885): In this Aberdeen photo printing works, about 85 per cent of the workers are women.

from food to civil engineering. Models have a short employment span, but some move on into the management of agencies. The exploitative relationship between women and photography is not simply one-way. Even so, the photography industry does considerably better out of women than vice-versa.[14]

Overall, the place of women in professional photography has changed very little since the Victorian era, as the Grunwick photographic strike in London in 1977 illustrated.[15] However, by the mid-seventies, it was not simply that the majority of the striking workers were women, they were Asians, women from the even more disadvantaged and poorly paid immigrant community. The worldwide ubiquity of snap photography is underpinned by the low wages of thousands of relatively disempowered people – mainly women.

In the UK, the recent rapid expansion of this market has been based on mechanization, with a reduction of semi-skilled jobs in favour of a few skilled technicians (usually male) and some part-time unskilled packers and sorters (usually female).

When it comes to taking photos, things have changed a great deal since the 1840s. In those early times, it was only the most extraordinary women who combined the financial resources and doggedness necessary to take up photography as a hobby. The introduction of the wet-plate in the early 1850s made little difference to women's participation in photography. Julia Margaret Cameron is an example of the extra-ordinary women who could break with the dominant ideology of Victorian society to make photos.[16] Whilst there was a space for the male scientist-artist-eccentric in Victorian society, there generally wasn't an equivalent space for a female.

The dry-plate of the late 1870s or early 1880s made a difference, in as much as it was considered more 'ladylike', but the real barriers to women's involvement were the social arrangements of the time. Men controlled the finances and made the decision to buy a camera to document their lives. Father would take the pictures, mother and children would present 'the family' to the camera. Later, as the patriarchal nature of the family changed, mother became able to voice her opinion on when events were worth photographing, but children got the camera in their hands before mothers did. Mums always have other assumed responsibilities; controlling the kids, seeing to the meal and so on.

The low wages of single women meant that, whilst ahead of mothers in the queue to take the photographs, they lagged behind single males, families and children. It is rare for there to exist any participant images of young female peer group activity before the Second World War, and after the war these were recorded much less frequently than the single male's peer group pursuits.

Female peer group (circa 1942): **This Land Army picture is typical of the female peer group photos often precipitated out of the newly experienced collectivity of the war effort.**

The great change has been since the 1960s. The increase in women's job opportunities has been coupled with a decrease in wage differentials. Changes in patterns of assumptions about family relationships have also played their part. Nowadays, until about the age of 35, women are as likely as men to take photos. It is when mum is saddled with the responsibilities of bringing kids up that dad and older children take over.[17]

A note on histories

Short historical overviews like this inevitably simplify the way cultural practices change. They isolate events and take them out of context so as to present them as ordered elements in a narrative of reduced complexity. This reduction is always based on unexamined assumptions – and never more so than when claiming natural or scientific underpinnings. In short, potted histories encourage the sorts of conflation that cultural studies aims to highlight and examine. For this reason, historical essays in the emerging tradition of cultural studies tend to be detailed and to concentrate on cases which it is hoped will prove pivotal, or at least emblematic.[18] In the space available here it was not possible to enter into this sort of detail.

Obviously, any history must be partial. This short history of amateur photography as a popular cultural activity is no exception. However, it has been attempted to make it usefully partial by concentrating on aspects of the changes in vernacular photography which are seldom given a high profile. For more detailed, and often conflicting treatments, please refer to the works cited in the notes.

2 The albums

When people are asked what they photograph, a general list emerges. 'Families' and 'holidays' come out on top, (somewhat interchangeably) and then subject categories such as 'people', 'nature', 'buildings' and 'hobbies' follow, roughly in that order.[1] These categories overlap, and some complete categories may be subsumed under others, (e.g. 'people' may be largely included in 'families'). However, within these uncertain categories some fairly firm assertions can be made. The most popular human subjects for parents are their children. Runners up in this poll are partners and then grandchildren.[2]

If we dig behind our reasons for taking photos, another list emerges. We mainly take pictures to support our memories. We also want to represent our personal relationships with those dear to us. Then we want records of our involvement with the physical environment. Many of our answers can be understood as being underpinned by concerns for aesthetic pleasure, (although we don't volunteer this motivation straight out). That is, we want to record beauty. Similarly, a concern to manage some of our emotional experience via snap photography emerges from such statements as: 'I take photos to evoke mood and help focus emotions.'[3]

It is possible to see two sorts of criteria emerging from the judgements we make of our photographs. Firstly, there are personal criteria by which we want our photos to be, 'happy', 'fun', 'not boring' and to 'bring back memories'. Secondly, more public criteria include, 'well composed', 'technically good', 'imaginative' and 'interesting'.[4]

It is possible to analyse our reasons for seeing something as photographable or not. It seems that in making these decisions we are weighing things up on four scales of suitability which can be described as follows:

1. Is it socially acceptable?
2. Is is public or private?
3. Is it socially meaningful, or primarily of aesthetic interest?
4. Is it unique, or an everyday occurrence?

Whilst we show a good deal of idiosyncrasy in how we arrive at our judgements of photogenic situations and the photos that result from them, we are much more likely to agree in our conclusions.[5]

The variations we exhibit in our thinking about photographs don't seem to link up with any general characteristics we may have. The amount of photography we do, how long we have done it for, what our other interests are, what sex we are, how old we are; none of these seem to correlate reliably with how we understand photography.[6] However, some links do occur. Men are more likely to be interested in the technical side of photography, but those that are do not necessarily have anything else in common. What does link strongly to our vernacular photography is our wider social experience. This becomes clearer when dealing with the categories of vernacular photography on pages 25 to 63.

Within the household group there is often a 'main photographer', someone who is keener than the rest and takes most of the photos. Often these people concentrate on photographing their hobbies, or on photography *as* a hobby. In these circumstances, the domestic vernacular photographs described later in this chapter may be left to others in the household, (with certain exceptions, e.g. the most 'formal' and the least domestic).[7]

One thing we use domestic photography for is to signal to ourselves (whether knowingly or not) certain experiences as important. This importance can be personal or cultural, and these aspects may be reinforced by virtue of being different to the everyday, or by being the underlying dependables of our lives. Such photography celebrates our successes. It also helps make our emotional lives tangible, and combats the psychological effects of distance and passing time, bringing us closer together and sustaining our fleeting pleasures.

But these positive factors have another side to them. They leave important aspects of experience out of the account – everyday drudgery, the unpleasant or threatening experience, illness, discord. These are all factors affecting who we are. What is more, their absence disguises the realities of the domestic power struggles which go on around us. To put it at its most extreme, could we have turned a blind eye to child abuse and domestic violence for so long, if it had featured in our family albums? Perhaps photos would have been an effective prophylactic, given some families repetition of abuse down through the generations.

Family photography doesn't actively lie about our experience, rather its sin is that of omission. Even the choice of positive experience to be celebrated must leave other viewpoints unexpressed; the child is depicted by dad, 'reaching up for mummy', the scene has pathos for the adults and evokes compassion at every viewing. For the child, the powerlessness and gulf of misunderstanding realized at the moment of frustration may come flooding back when the photo is seen.[8] In certain circumstances, even the most cheerful image may recall the darker side of family life to its members.[9]

These possible contradictions can be used to explore to the full

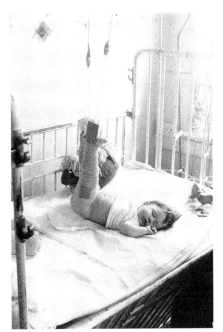

Illness: An exception to the general embargo on photographs of illness is when full recovery is confidently expected. Indeed, if the 'illness' is remedial medical attention, the expected outcome is an improvement over the prognosis without such 'illness'/hospitalization. In these circumstances, photographs document the hopeful beginnings of a new life.

Baby: Even at this early age, families may see characteristic attitudes in a child's picture, and see it as a 'typical' picture (see 'That's typical' p. 27).

the messages vernacular photography conceals [see chapter five].

Leaving behind what is *not* depicted, the rest of this chapter deals with what *is*. My categorizations of photo albums' content have arisen out of in-depth interviews with vernacular photographers and discussions of their albums, together with a need to address the social forces that impinge upon leisure and everyday life.

The albums, part one: family

Vernacular photography is about exploring our personal experience through picturing. Family photography is about picturing our close personal relationships.

Babies: Most parents love their babies. At the very least they function for us symbolically as condensed points of personal experience and relationships. The sense of responsibility, and the strength of emotions precipitated, make the baby a must for photography. The firstborn will be most provocative of new experience, and as such 'demands' more photos than subsequent children. (This may not occur in certain cases – if the firstborn is the 'wrong' gender, is handicapped, or belongs to some other socially suppressed group, for example.) As children put a strain on the household budget, subsequent offspring may be photographed less because of the cost. (This is less a factor in the West where photography is relatively cheap.)

Mother and baby: Such photos are in part the vernacular culmination of a long lineage stretching back at least to the Madonna and Child illustrations of medieval Christianity. As such they draw upon assumptions which place the mother and child in a direct relationship with God and Nature. Prior to the Enlightenment this relationship placed women and children in the universal hierarchy. In this hierarchy God gave his authority to the king, who bestowed it upon his nobles, who devolved it to free men. Wives were placed in this 'Chain of Being' by virtue of bearing heirs.[10] Something of this venerability acquired through motherhood remains for wives.

In our culture, women are generally most involved with child rearing, indeed society always ultimately holds them *responsible* for it.[11] Most women are brought up to be mothers and experience great fulfilment in, and exhibit deep love for their babies. So it *seems* 'natural' that mothers should be photographed with their babies much more frequently than fathers. It is also usually the case that fathers have annexed the camera by the time parenthood comes along.[12] Besides, mum normally has her 'hands full' with the baby and is too busy coping to take the pictures.

Father and baby: Such pictures do occur; often they are taken after the 'mother and baby' pose, in a spirit of equality and mutual (but different) involvement. Sometimes they are taken because dad is amusing the child, and this is sufficiently special to warrant a photo.

Mother and baby: Ultimately children are their mother's responsibility in our culture, unless a nanny is employed.

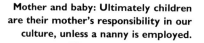

Dads and diapers: As more and more couples attempt to share the burdens of parenting, some fathers become caught up in the stresses of child-rearing. Although not at all common, the scenario by which the exception to the rule is photographable (even if it is a societal rule, not a family one) may result in some photos which do not depict dad as the playmate, but as a carer.

More and more this 'dad amusing the baby' is typical of the father's involvement with child rearing, and as such warrants a photo in the same fashion as the mother's 'special' relationship (with the important difference of a *lack* of responsibility for nurture).

In both 'parents and baby' photos there is an aspect of personal meaning which is perhaps less acceptable. Babies are generally seen as achievements; both as tangible symbols of commitment to a loving relationship and as success in procreating life. They are also like a form of property, as they share the attributes of potential economic value, subjugation (of a sort) to our will and symbolism of achievement. They also require us to be responsible for them. This 'property-ness' of babies may lurk in the shadows of any baby photo.

'That's typical!': In our collection of family snaps there will be some presenting the 'typical' actions of its members. These 'that's typical!' pictures are of two types. There is the typical reaction to being photographed: Dad grins stupidly, junior acts the fool and the tousle-headed little girl peers sheepishly from half closed eyes (later cited as early indications of her coquettishness?). These photos usually display the power relations of the family because they are often taken of the socially weak by the relatively powerful. They can (and must) define the attributes of the family members. Initially children and mothers will have their 'typicalities' recorded in the album – later they get their own back.

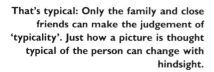

That's typical: Only the family and close friends can make the judgement of 'typicality'. Just how a picture is thought typical of the person can change with hindsight.

Secondly, there are those 'typical' photos which are taken specifically to document and comment upon repeated facets of a close relative or friend. These may also be of two sorts. There are typical role activities that the photographer may catch: offspring 'studying' with stereo headphones pumping loud music into their heads, parents at domestic work, or asleep in front of the TV. These photos may be celebratory and signify loving acknowledgement of the family's social relations, or they can be ironic comments on the tensions of family life.

The second sort of 'typical personal facet' photo is that which records individual quirks: characteristic personality traits as revealed through actions, or a certain posture or look. 'Typical' actions by virtue of role or character traits can change their label with time. Falling asleep in front of a favourite 'soap' may be understood as a personal quirk by the photographer, and recorded as such. Later, an awareness of the exhaustion engendered by a demanding social role may develop in the family. If so, such napping may then be understood in terms of this role. Most of our typicalities have close relationships with role demands. Conversely, this confusion between role and personality can become so integrated in the fabric of the household and the person that the role position becomes a quirk. Any one photo can be seen as ironic, celebratory, role specific or characteristic of personality according to the understandings of the viewer and the state of family relationships at the time.

Rites of passage: Birthdays, christenings, confirmation, celebrations of attaining adulthood, graduation from a course of training, marriage, or birth: these events are celebrated in most cultures and are musts for vernacular photography. The rites themselves place us in time and society. Photographs of these events both prove our attainments and enable the celebration to exist tangibly in our social world beyond the normal limits of its space and time. Such photos were amongst the earliest ever taken and remain the staple of High Street photography. The formality of the professional portraits confers dignity upon us and for many families, some formal dignity on these occasions is preferred. (Regardless of our personal concerns, that we 'look awful', that 'it's not me' and so on.)

Important possessions: We develop deep relationships with certain possessions. For children, some toys take on special significance. They invest them with individual personalities (dolls, soft toys) or magical powers (the penknife that is an interstellar communicator and ray gun). When children photograph these possessions, it would seem to be part of simply recognizing their importance for them. At the same time they apparently concretize their fantasies as embodied in the possessions. In the case of toys as surrogate friends, children can exercise their developing social skills by returning the compliment of the toy's interest and forebearance and taking (or having someone else take) a photo of their 'friend'.

The practice continues into adulthood. Certain possessions are so ubiquitous in our albums that they need consideration in their own right: house, car, and boat photos are cases in point. We also photograph possessions that are more descriptive of ourselves than

Rites of passage: Without knowing the context of this image, it seems just a gender swap of the car possession photo ('Adult With Car', p. 31). However, I do know that the woman has the car by virtue of her job as a teacher of the blind, and it symbolizes her access to the status of the post. The 'caring professions' have relied on women's commitment and their training in the family as would-be mothers – the ultimate carer's role. This devotion to caring is seldom rewarded by such a tangible emblem of achievement.

Childhood possessions: Important objects feature prominently in children's photos. Sometimes a child's most important possession is an invisible playmate, so they have to make do with photos of second best.

First bike: As general affluence increases, the recipients get younger. Since the 1960s the teen market has exploded and its influence in terms of fashion and consumer desire has spread down the years to five-year-olds. The first 'real' bike still marks a stage of independence, but it is not *the* symbol of entering adolescence it used to be.

Insurance photos: Enigmatic without the knowledge of their purpose.

these widely shared icons. This is usually motivated by that special relationship that combines vestiges of childhood magic and fantasy with showing off consumer expertise and purchasing power – which is constantly promoted as success by advertisers.

Two other kinds of possession photographs appear in photo albums. Firstly, people with whom we have personal relationships (especially those who are separated from us by distance or time) are rekindled in our thoughts by objects which are specially associated with them. Secondly, ordinary people are taking more and more photos for insurance purposes. (Perhaps because in modern society we are increasingly concerned about perceived lawlessness, and also the incompatability of our long term financial committments with nature's vicissitudes.) These documents are fascinating because they seem to flout the usual norms of vernacular photography. Consumer durables are decontextualized and are often indistinguishable from their millions of brethren. Most intriguing are those images showing the result of natural 'disaster', intended to back up an insurance claim. Without the contextual knowledge of the written claim the garden walls, house roofs, windows, doors, leaning trees and trape-zoid garages take on a surrealist aesthetic worthy of seventies art photography.

Child and bike: This is a recurrent image in vernacular photography. As an industrial product, bicycles run parallel to cameras in the history of their invention, ownership and distribution through society. Cabinet photos of the 1880s would depict young men (and later, aspiring young women – see p. 14) confidently grasping the bars of a bike. It was, and still remains, the first symbol of independence and achievement. Getting the first real bike is a rite of passage for today's child. Previously, baby strollers, trikes and non-road bikes may be photographed by parents with undertones of encouragement for the child's burgeoning independence, but the first real bike is the culmination of childhood.

Adult with car: Again, this marks a modern rite of passage; this time, out of, rather than into, adolescence. However, in the past cars were not immediately affordable by most people. Older photos show the now familiar story of the car appearing almost exclusively with a wealthy male, and then the gradual dispersal of ownership through the classes, across genders and to all ages allowed to drive. Car ownership used to be a mark of social status. Photos 'proving' ownership acted like membership cards, calling forth the initiate's argot. Arcane mechanical lore could be exchanged and tall stories related. In these days, when mass production has made cars ordinary, boat ownership, and photos of them, may fulfil the same function.

Grandpa's car: If you'd been an agricultural labourer at the turn of the century, wouldn't you be proud to own such an opulent and rounded car?

House: The house features in many vernacular photos, as the frame of a view, as the subject of an insurance claim [see p. 30] and most often, simply as the context for a social event. But the house photo also shares a mode very similar to the car, boat or bicycle snap. Although this function is in decline, the house is still depicted as a symbol of successful familial provision. For the immigrant, or those struggling free of subsistence wages, the first secure accommodation

This is where granny lives: As with insurance photos, some of these house/window shots are inexplicable without information from the photographer. Here the space associated with a special person is celebrated. This is the view from grandmother's kitchen window, as she stands by the sink.

is especially a matter of relief and pride.

A variant of the house photo is the one through the window to outside [above]. This celebrates a view. Often such photos are less about what that view consists of, than about the occupation of the space inside which commands it. In a structure of vision which echoes the land ownership paintings of the seventeenth to nineteenth centuries, we make a concrete representation of our 'place' in the world, both our rights to occupation and our resultant responsibilities.[13]

Anyone with a camera can celebrate their physical relations to the immediate geography. Children celebrate their bedroom via its window's view, families their home via their dining room view.

Meals: This is another subject where we can celebrate our ability to provide for ourselves. The formal meal itself has long had these associations. The mid-winter Christmas banquet has strong connotations of brazen consumption in the face of mean times.

Of similar symbolic importance is the condensation of family structure. Coming together around a table brings relatives into close proximity almost naturally. So arranged, they can all fall into the frame for the record of the unitary family. In a manner reminiscent of the coat of arms or the highland tartan, the celebratory meal photo is a talisman of belonging. It concretizes the complex bonds of heredity, indebtedness and familiarity and encourages our integration into the tribe [see p. 55].

Such formal meals may condense the family structure socially as well as spatially. The head of the household may still sit at the 'head' of the table with siblings arranged at his/her right or left hand, according to favour. When such structures have been forsaken, their absence becomes in itself a statement of egalitarian masquerade.

So, the combination of familial plenty and integration makes the celebration of the family meal a powerful symbol and it is not surprising that it crops up in various guises throughout photo albums.

Dining out: This is a special case of the family meal photo. Usually the event signifies a special occasion and the photo marks it as such. The formal arrangement of people (couples side-by-side, the patriarch at the head of the table) is often accomplished by the restaurant staff.

Hobbies: In the UK, photography is thought to be the third most popular pastime behind shopping and gardening.[14] Although photos associated with photography do appear, it is sports which form the largest sub-group of hobby photos. Mountains of research have been done into the relations between people and their sporting/leisure pursuits.[15] Sports fulfil complex psychological and social functions for those involved. Photography can immortalize their successes, objectify their failures; and for the vast majority of non-competitor spectators, enable vicarious involvement to be heightened and made tangible.

Other hobby photos display similar orientations, with shots of prize givings and competition entries much in evidence.

Dressing up: Generally it appears that once an event such as 'dressing up' is deemed suitable for photography within a close social

Hobbies/sports: A photo which combines team, trophy and sport. The tug-o-war team photo-snatched between work responsibilities, hence the variation in levels of dress. A photocall with more notice would have brought out the Sunday best.

grouping, then this event will be regularly documented and its suitability as a subject (even necessity) passed on within the group. This dissemination seems particularly evident with pictures of possessions such as teddy bears, bikes and boats.

When it comes to 'dressing up photos', we are fascinated by the changes wrought upon familiar persons. They become funny, newly attractive, or just odd. For the person in costume, the reason for dressing up may well be important, perhaps part of a hobby. A photograph records the event via the costume and acknowledges its importance. The costume itself may well have been the result of much skilled DIY effort, and a photo acknowledges this too.

Official photos: Except for the first twenty years, most vernacular photography was 'official' until after World War Two. It recorded, in a pseudo-legalistic manner, social functions of relative importance. The probative nature of such photography is evident in today's rites of passage photographs [see pp. 28–9]. Nowadays such photographs are still required for our interface with the powerful institutions of society. The school photo is likely to be our first

The school photo: A 1930s infants school. Itinerant photographers travelled districts recording children at school. The long school photo of hundreds of children was only common after WW2. Individual images for the child's educational dossier came to Britain in the sixties.

encounter with this mode of representation. But it continues with graduation and 'in uniform' photos. Here we must present the image of a model human.

Sibling games: There is always a tendency to look back on childhood as a simpler and purer time. The adults look at such photos of their children, now grown, and wonder what might have been. The children in later life remember an uncomplicated world of direct emotion, and may be moved to nostalgia or embarassment at the remembrance of such naivety. When kids photograph themselves at play, the action becomes part of the play. The photographer coaxes and cajoles, whilst the subjects posture, play the fool, and borrow from the TV, with action replays and demonstrations for the camera. By their actions children show their awareness of the importance of taking a photo. The everyday and mundane is not good enough. Normal play is abandoned for special 'photographic

Kids at play: The adult photographer stands above the children and captures the delightful scene. This photo was taken on the south coast of England in the 1970s – at a time when the apparent harmony between black and white would have been recordable as white liberal adults became aware of an influx of other races from London and further afield. They hoped for harmony and integration; this photo could be a talisman to that end.

play'. In later life an awareness of the camera is often what comes most frequently to the subject's mind when reliving the scene via a photo.

Spouse: Photos of partners abound in albums, though they are often severely edited. Ex-spouses may be expunged and there are seldom embarrasing ones of old flames. Given that we normally don't destroy photos, this may point to an interesting area. When crossed in love, we do destroy or discard photos of the guilty party. Indeed, removing tangible reminders of our folly may be an important part of starting anew. If the split has been without rancour, do we just 'mislay' the photos, which then sink unnoticed from our lives?

Partner photos have meaningful peaks and troughs of frequency. We start out in our relationships by photographing the object of our desires fairly frequently. Indeed, photography may be part of the modern mating ritual [see p. 37]. With the advent of children in a relationship, fathers turn their attention to the offspring. Or at least, their partner becomes an inseparable part of the mother/child team and less a subject in her own right. Mothers are likely to have given up photography before children are an issue.[16] The development of a relationship involves the negotiation of roles for each partner, and

Spouse: Early holidays without children are peaks of partner photography.

the role of 'official recorder' is often given over to the male, even though the decision to record may remain a co-operative, even female-dominated area.[17]

At present most photographers are over 40 years old[18] and they use their cameras to record outings. The partner photograph is revived in these later years as they are depicted standing in front of landmarks and the like.

Grandchildren: Given that the majority of active amateur photographers are beyond childrearing age, young children might be assumed not to figure prominently in their repertoire. This is not the case; vernacular photography is full of pictures of grandchildren.

The financial gains of mature people (epitomized in the American term 'the silver economy') seem likely to give rise to more leisure pursuit aimed at them. These may reorientate some older people away from almost exclusively family-based leisure.

This could affect the classes differently because, despite the aforementioned gains for some, old people receiving only state pensions are amongst the poorest in our society. They will still have no alternative to family-oriented leisure, because it is usually the cheapest.

Young parents can now afford to document their offspring's every move. Their abundance of kid photos, combined with changes in leisure activity for some in the silver economy may result in people having less of a desire to photograph their grandchildren. At the

Grandparents and children: Guiltless revisitation of parenthood.

moment, however, it shows no sign of wavering in popularity.

Whilst both grandparents can photographically celebrate having provided sufficiently for their children to be able to support their own children [see pp. 27 and 31], there are gendered differences to grandparenthood which can underlie these shots. Currently, most mature photographers are male and were fathers at a time when heavy involvement in childrearing for men was generally considered irregular. Now, as grandparents they are distanced from the problems of the division of childrearing responsibilities and its accompanying mixture of desire and guilt. Grandfathers can have the good parts of young children (cuddles, games, 'spoiling rotten') without the risk of responsibility for the unpleasant, grinding work-aday side arising. Vernacular photography documents this guiltless revisitation of fatherhood.

Grandmothers can photograph their grandchildren instead of being responsible for them every minute, as most were when mothers. So such photography can stem from the deep understand-ing they have of children (gained at the expense of motherhood's responsibilities), whilst simultaneously celebrating the new freedom of parenting one step removed.

Girl/boyfriend: Photography involves looking and necessarily, ack-nowledging the fact of looking. The photo endorses, amplifies and concretizes the act. Looking at the opposite sex is frequently con-fused with sexual interest (by both looker and looked at). If we include the fact that taking a photo is a sign of interest and value, we can see why photography might figure in modern courtship. Through taking photos we can make contact with those we are comfortable with/attracted to, without risking our egos by rejection.

Boy/girfriends figure in our vernacular photography in another way: as embarassed (and embarassing) audience. Prospective partners must at sometime be brought back to the parental nest, where the photo album lurks in the shadows. Its embarassment potential lies in the fact that the images depict us as others saw us, we were not in control of our presentation of self [see p. 41].

Introducing the family: This photo is a cheat on my part. It doesn't depict a boyfriend being subjected to the family album, but a cousin. We don't photograph such potentially difficult situations, it wouldn't be fair on the new initiate. However, for those of us who have been through it, I expect the image recalls the moment.

Finding and getting along with a partner is at least partly about controlling how we present ourselves, and mutually negotiating changes in this presentation. The family album can be something of a threat to these negotiations. How these images of a relatively powerless past (at best unconsidered, at worst undermining) are negotiated by the prospective partner is a minor milestone in a developing relationship.

Friends: Because vernacular photography is about bestowing tokens of value on our experience, the experience of friendship is bound to be reflected in our photo collection. The photos we take begin by depicting the family and its domain. Then in pre-adolescence friends begin to appear, and by adolescence, often predominate. Anyone who has looked at a niece or nephew's photo collection knows the experience of confronting a stream of unknown faces, whose significance obviously goes beyond the names which the youngster enthusiastically recounts.

In late adolescence photos of friends become more discriminating, best friends recur, but the wider circle dwindles.

Early adulthood is often a time when we are separated from our background and childhood circle of friends. Photos reflect this. It is also around this time that the mating game comes into its own, and photos reflect this, too.

Finally photography comes back to concentrating on the family, though this time *our own* family. With the exception of committed amateurs who may use friends as models to perfect their portrait technique, most take photos of 'friends' met fleetingly on holiday and never seen again. Generally, photographing real friends may occur through recording a mutual leisure interest, not because they're friends.

Peer group photo: These photos at least partly depict our 'other families'. Relationships in the associations we belong to are family-

Peer group photos: Society groups us together at various times in our lives, and in different institutions. Common ones are the armed forces and educational institutions. Often these are single sex institutions.

like in terms of possible levels of involvement, emotional saturation and mutual indebtedness. Peer group photos acknowledge this connectedness and record the faces of surrogate families for future bouts of reminiscence. Many of these associations have firmly enforced structures and they generate 'official photos' [see p. 34]. These are kept more because of the characters behind the uniforms (imposed or assumed) than the official status of the images. Indeed, the controlled nature of the official record may call to mind those occasions when the group or its members were least controlled, and after the event we thought 'what a picture that would've made!'

The visitor's picture: When visitors come to the household, the camera is likely to be in evidence. Often the favoured visitor is asked to take a picture of the family. These pictures are interesting because they often have a strange air about them, somewhat heightened. Families 'act up for the camera', a bit more for the visitor. The photo modelled on the formal document [see p. 54] is more formal

Visitor photos: This is a found photo, so I can't really be sure that it *is* a visitor photo, but given the acting up for the camera, and the jokey role reversal, it certainly could be.

than if produced without the visitor's aid. The informal photo is more 'larky' – more 'acting the fool' goes on. When visitors are staying a family group 'puts on a face' to an extent and this is recorded in such photos.

Sex: Apparently quite a bit of 'sexy' shooting goes on in the vernacular. Postal print houses pass thousands of such photos through their impersonal print lines.[19] Possible relationships between sexual desire and the specialized looking involved in photography are the subject of some debate within psychology,[20] but that the two can be combined in erotica and pornography is obvious from these forms' longevity and unbiquity.

In vernacular 'sexy partner' photography, the usual questions of power, control and negotiation (always at issue in human relationships), must be to the fore. However, such photos don't usually get lumped in with the general collection. They are not for a wider public than the two people involved, but as ever, they document and celebrate important personal experience. It is just that these experiences are not to be more widely shared. Their purpose is to retain ('out of time') fleeting but vivid experience, and to heighten this by representing it in concrete signs.

Pets: As far as vernacular photos are concerned, pets are members of the family and appear as such. For children especially, some of their closest relationships are with pets. They photograph them because they love them; and because the pets can't refuse [see p. 72].

Children do not have the necessary power over adults to command them to be photographed (although in Western cultures they *do* have considerable power over adults, it is not that of command). Pets however are never 'too busy' or 'looking dreadful'. Because the relationship of a child to its pet may be very deep, the quality of the photo is often far less important than its existence as a memento of the subject. Children often have fixed-focus cameras with minimum focus distances of five feet; these are simple and cheap, but they are useless for images of small pets taken from distances reflecting the closeness of a child's relationship. We have all seen the abstract blur (given pride of place by the child) which we are told is 'Tiddles'.

Women with pets: Not as discussed in the text, but remarkably similar to the article discussed in Chapter Three. Often adults 'play' with pets for the camera. It is one way of keeping the animal under control for the photo.

Another sort of pet photo depicts a person and a pet. Apart from the child and pet photos pictured by a parent, there is a significant subgenre which shows women with pets. This would seem to arise from the demarcation of labour in Western society which left women in the house, whilst men went out.[21] In this set-up, the woman's constant companion (and in a sense, proxy partner) was the pet. This relationship was overlaid by the tradition of caring mothers and the role of the pet as surrogate offspring (at least, prior to parenthood). Thus there are millions of photos of women holding house cats in a duplicate of the place and pose that they hold their firstborn elsewhere in the album.

Acting the fool: All over the field of vernacular photography we 'act the fool', undermining the formal photo and acting up for the casual group. All the photographic modes – 'holiday', 'wedding' and so on (with the exception of 'serious amateur' photography) show copious examples of 'larking about'. To understand this we need to go back to what it feels like to be photographed.

As soon as we become aware that we are about to be photographed, we realize that we don't know how we look (prior to a photo we will check our reflections if possible). What is more, we also don't know what to do to communicate via the photo *who* we are. This results in the decision to 'pose'. Any presentation of self before the camera is partial, and we must make a choice of which part to present. These choices are undermined by an awareness of our lack of control over self-presentation. The situation is admirably described by Roland Barthes,[22] who says of our choice of action: 'I pose, I know I am posing, I want you to know that I am posing, but (to square the circle) this additional message must in no way alter the precious essence of my individuality' [ibid. p. 11].

Halla Beloff[23] has made the connection between this onset of awareness – of being 'on the spot' and of sending it up. She calls this the 'anti-pose'. Often the gap between the degree of importance we attach to being 'captured' at the time and our lack of control over how we will appear is too great for us to choose to be partially reflected in the pose. In these circumstances we undermine any

Larking about: See text and picture on p. 53.

Acting the fool: 'I'm acting the fool, and I want you to know it!'

attempt at a definitive 'us', and act the fool, choosing to show our awareness of the photograph and our distance from any attempt at revelation. To echo Barthes: 'I act the fool, I know I am acting the fool, I am sure you will know that I am acting the fool and I know this additional message will protect my individuality by alluding to a plenitude of "me" elsewhere.'

In the family such anti-poses are frequent, partly because we know how partial revelation can be used to fix our supposed character in the form of 'that's typical!' [see p. 27] but also because the family already has a grasp of our true complexity. This can be relied upon to rescue us from our embarassment, and so the anti-pose is a favoured act of awareness under threat of photography.

Displaying agility/strength:A significant subject of vernacular photos depict young people displaying their acrobatic or athletic prowess. This is a combination of celebrating their mastery of physical skills, acting the fool and showing-off. The element of physical skill celebration is somewhat like displaying the biggest fish caught, or the cup won; youngsters display the symbols of their achievement. Burgeoning physical skills are symbolized by the cartwheel or handstand, as fishing skills are symbolized by the big fish.

Additionally, this act for the camera is a good example of another typical pre-adolescent response to difficulties in the presentation of self and its reading by others: 'showing-off'. Most of us at this age have tried to use 'showing off', in circumstances where a relative

'LOOK AT ME!': Showing off in the nicest possible way.

stranger, who is deemed important by our family, visits and we feel the need to create an impression and yet not allow ourselves to be vulnerable.

The albums, part two: Christmas photos

Women's photos: It is almost obligatory to take photos at Christmas (in Judeo-Christian cultures). The festival has pre-Christian connections to feasting and a heightened awareness of social bonding. The modern Christmas has retained and enlarged on this. Such vernacular photographic genres as 'the family meal', 'extended family' and 'games' are condensed into a short period of heightened emotionality.

Superficially, women's lack of involvement in vernacular photography is apparent from the infrequency of their camera usage and the overwhelmingly male orientation of the amateur market [see chapter three and p. 92]. However, it is at Christmas that the underlying truths of women's involvement begin to become apparent. There is the familiar scenario in which 'the woman of the household' buys film at the supermarket whilst stocking up for Christmas. Then, when the holiday period starts, she makes sure the camera is loaded (though not necessarily by her) and available to document the festivities that have fallen to her to arrange. During the festivities, she will probably not take the pictures, being too busy with other things (or even enjoying a rest) and anyway, probably unfamiliar with that role and its technology. However, she will

Young women take photos: Prior to a certain age, women are as likely to take photos as men. The likelihood is reduced with the onset of parenting, but who decides when a photo is required is another story.

prompt other household members to take pictures. After all, it is she who has invested most in the events of Christmas, whether she likes it or not.[24] Women are not uninvolved with vernacular photography, it is just that our narrow criteria for what constitutes involvement – taking the photo – is too limiting when it comes to trying to understand the cultural experience.

Presents: Photos of giving and receiving presents are a special sub-

Christmas presents: See text.

genre of possession photos. Presents themselves are not just tokens of affection, but are also messages of social indebtedness as well as connection. We may not love uncle George, but: if aunt Georgina got one, if he always gives us one, if we're to figure in his will … and so on.

We record this ritual exchange for reasons similar to house and other possession photos [see pp. 29–32], and of course because most of us enjoy the activity. We smile, and the kids look in wonderment as they receive and open their gifts; and this makes for excellent photos of our fantasy happy family life.[25] Such a ritual is the epitome of successful 'family-ness'. Even if it is all on credit and only lasts till after lunch biliousness, this doesn't matter. We are dealing with the important matters here – social metaphors, not those irritating material facts of economic distress and associated domestic friction. Next year these realities will be forgotten and the myth will reign again – at least till after lunch.

Santa: The 'child with Santa' photo may have been initiated in the department stores of the USA, during the 1920s. This genre has its

Santa: This photo is interesting because it was in the collection of the Santa, not the child. Whilst work seldom figures in family albums (unless outside, where nature intervenes, see pp. 57–62, or when play is mixed with work), such voluntary work is much more likely to appear.

precursor in the formulaic *carte-de-visites* of the 1860s. In Santa photos we have a similar formulaic set up. The production line of Victorian *carte* photography [see p. 13] is echoed by the in-store Santa photo. The children's magical event, 'seeing Santa Claus', is recorded on the department store photo conveyor belt.

In-store photography seems to have declined recently, possibly because amateurs themselves can duplicate the child and Santa photo with the thousands of itinerant Santas to be found advertising charities and so on. They can also easily take all manner of 'child at Christmas' photos that used to be less possible, due to technical difficulty and expense in the past. Interior photos were not easy for amateurs until the general availability of flash in the fifties and sixties.

Parties: We photograph parties whenever they occur. But children's and old people's parties are favoured, alongside of the family Christmas 'do'.

Photography can capture fun for recirculation after the event [see pp. 94–5]. It can mark high spots of the celebrations, helping to create a rhythm of exuberance. It can be used to organize party-goers and promote socializing. It can also be used as a way for those who feel slightly outside the festivities to be involved, to have a party role. By the same token, it can be used to separate party-goers from what otherwise might call for too much involvement. Photography is first and foremost an act and like any other act, it takes its meaning not only from internal coherence but also from its performance and context. The act of photography can be used in as many ways as a smile. Of course, if we're having a really good time, we forget about photos altogether!

Party: See text.

The albums, part three: holidays

Window: This subject is one of the earliest in holiday photos[26] and continues to crop up frequently in albums. When on holiday, it is often the first one taken. Travelling to holiday destinations can be a stressful experience. Rushing to make departure times, keeping the party together (both spatially and psychologically) and being stuck in claustrophobic mass travel vehicles, builds up tension, mixed with the excitement and apprehension of the unknown. On reaching the end of the journey, we feel different. We are in the 'holiday space'; the anticipated land to which we've sacrificed the journey, (and a sizeable portion of our spare income). A photo of the view from the window can mark this feeling of arrival. 'Getting there' is over and the holiday experience lies 'out there', ready to be seized with open arms.

Holiday window: To a degree, the content of the view does not matter, what's important is that you have it, and it's different.

New landscapes: Photos of the unfamiliar landscape are practically obligatory in the holiday album. Not just a reminder of the scenery (exotic because different), these photos are also proof of travel and can score highly in the games of 'competitive experience collecting' and 'living life successfully'. These photos also mark our arrival in 'holiday land' and enable us to give tangible acknowledgment to our experience of being 'away' from our everyday geography with its accompanying social position. Often we place ourselves, or members of our party; in front of the landscape, proving our involvement with the experience of magical 'holiday land'.

Here we are: See 'New landscapes'.

New buildings: Not all the buildings photographed on holiday are officially designated sites for sightseers [see p. 53]. Many architectural photographs are similar to those of the unfamiliar landscape. They prove our attendance in an unfamiliar, interesting world. But more than the landscapes (at least for those of us inexperienced in agriculture) buildings speak of their inhabitants. Differences in architecture recall the possible differences between us and our fellow man. Suburbia, the victim of international non-style, does not feature in our holiday building snaps. But buildings in small towns or city centres set us snapping away. Accommodation, shops, even offices are the subjects for photos when they display stylistic difference to our experience at home. These buildings are not just different in their own right, they symbolize both the similarities of 'holiday land's inhabitants' (they too are home-workers, shoppers, workers), and their differences (they do these things in quaint, ugly, imposing, smart, dilapidated or 'odd' buildings).

The quaint and different: See 'New buildings'.

New social groups: After our initial experience of disorientation, we usually begin to establish a group of holiday friends. Photographs of the group and its members reflect the norms of domestic photography. We photograph the group at meals, messing about, relaxing etc. They may also be herded in front of the 'new landscape' or 'new building', to both prove our relation to them and the magical holiday experience, and to provide a cue for describing success in our social relationships when relating 'the story of the holiday'.

'This is us in the bar': See 'New social groups'.

Tour guide: See text.

Tour guide: A special sort of social record photo gets taken regularly on sightseeing coach tours. This is the photo of the courier, often standing by the coach. I don't know what proportion of these guides are women, but the majority of photos are taken of the female guides. These photos seem to combine several facets of both tours and amateur photography. The act of taking a photo is an indication of one's appreciation of the guide's service and pleasant disposition; in the world of vernacular photography, no one photographs the people they dislike. Furthermore, their position of employment means they are unlikely to refuse a request for a photo (like the amateur's domestic servant in pre-war photography [see p. 72]. The guides are usually attractive women, and as such fulfil a now traditional criterion for photogenic subjects [see p. 77–80]. The guide is also likely to be a local person and this adds to the extent to which our photographs can symbolically connect us to the inhabitants of 'holiday land'.

Picnic: The picnic photo depicts an event which joins together three important symbolic aspects of urban experience: nature, leisure and 'the meal' [see pp. 58–60]. These aspects of personal, psychological and social relations are photographed in their own right. When they all come together in the picnic, photography is a must! Holiday meals in general are a notable feature of our albums. They are exotic, because not our usual fare. They also feature our new peer group, condensed into one space, revelling in re-telling old jokes, drinking more than usual, and flirting.

Picnic: The meal, trees, nature, peer group. If you've got your camera, you must have a shot.

Holiday games: Play and games are essential holiday experiences. See text.

Local industry: Here glass engraving is shown off to the tourists in Portugal. Hopefully, by now these workers are wearing eye protection.

'Luvly!': Relaxing in the sun, see 'The seaside deckchair pose'.

Local activities: These are of two sorts. Firstly, those accidentally encountered and understood as interesting by virtue of comparison to our own versions of such pastimes (the neighbourhood kids playing soccer on a dust pitch surrounded with cacti). Secondly, the others that are presented as sights for sightseers. (Local festivals are an obvious example.) Local industries as tourist sights are perhaps most important to the local economy. The everyday goods made benefit from the extra commodity value created by becoming souvenirs. This manufacture may be advertised considerably and exist entirely for tourists, or they might be truly indigenous activities substantially unchanged by tourism. Dean MacCannel, an American sociologist, sees the move to ersatz activity for tourists as a stage in the progressive alienation of modern people from their experience. He argues that anthropological interest in other cultures' activities is rooted in a need to understand better our everyday experience.[27]

The seaside deckchair pose: I don't know if this is largely a British phenomenon, but collections frequently feature this sub-species of holiday photo. Getting a deckchair on an English beach was the culmination of arrival for the day's leisure experience. It symbolized journey's end. Also, like the condensation of the group around the meal table [see p. 32], deckchairs provide a static (and therefore, less technically demanding) spontaneous grouping. So, such photographs have about them something of the 'hotel window' [see p. 46] combined with the 'outing' [see pp. 52–3]. Add these factors to the increased likelihood of relaxed, embarrassing or 'typical' [see p. 52] poses that arise out of the ungainly deckchair, along with the sun's ability to create drowsiness; and we can understand something of the deckchair photo's ubiquity.

Seaside promenade: Another common sort of vernacular photo is that taken of people walking along the promenade or pier at a seaside resort. If we don't know the context of these photos, they just appear to be a person (or often a couple) walking down the street. Such photos were frequently taken by itinerant street photographers, who snapped on the off-chance that the subject would agree to order the result when accosted immediately afterwards. In Britain, this practice reached its height in the early 1950s, but with the increase of camera ownership following most people's improvement in conditions of work, speculative promenade photography faded out by the 1970s. In other countries where cameras are not so widespread but where photography is a part of the culture (notably in India and Thailand) speculative photography is still common.

In Britain this was considered to be a somewhat disreputable trade. Often the photographers were less skilled than their prices and confident attitude suggested and the results were disappointing when seen. Some young men used the camera mainly as an introduction to young women. Others were little better than confidence tricksters who took money before supplying any results. If these results were bad then the photographer would disappear from the seafront with the customer's deposits. A permanent booth, little or

There she was just walking down the street: See 'Seaside promenade'.

no deposit and an open manner were considered necessary credentials by the experienced holiday maker.

However, whatever the public standing of these photographers, it was a possible short term venture for the lively young man with few other prospects, especially the ex-serviceman with few civilian skills.

Camping: This special kind of holiday has a tradition going back to the early twentieth century. Whilst rambling and its associated camping was popular across the classes between the wars[28] currently, at the end of the century, it is primarily those needing a cheap break who take holidays under canvas: the young on low incomes, with no credit and no tradition of saving or those with large young families. These strictures become less evident if caravanning is included, partly because caravans and campervans cost money, but also because they tend to be more comfortable and their built-in mobility makes every weekend a potential holiday.[29]

The camping holiday produces all the types of familiar holiday photo: 'meals', 'landscapes', 'games' and so on, but it does have its own sub-genre, the 'tent photo'. This often echoes aspects of 'the window' and 'new landscapes' [see p. 46].

Boat trips: Somewhere in the typical album, there are always 'boat trip' photos. These are really just an obvious example of the more general 'travel-by-out-of-the-ordinary-modes-of-transport' photos. Boats, donkey carts, rickshaws and so on are all potential photo-subjects. These are almost obligatory if they are special sightseeing trips. They qualify for the camera on several counts. They are local activities inviting comparison with familiar modes of transport. The trips are taken to see sights and are part of that adventure. They are events in themselves – often the vehicles are decorated and the activity given a high profile in the area's advertising and tourists'

Camping: Often the tent appears about to fall down. Arriving in darkness, the tent is inexpertly pitched and the morning's light displays its crazy angles.

All aboard: Trains figure as a particular interest in the family which took this picture and so made this a must for photography. See 'Boat trips'.

general knowledge. Often the vehicle is a group transport machine, hence we have the 'new social group' squeezed into close proximity allowing those 'all of us' photos that would otherwise require cajoling and breaking the flow of holiday experience.

Characters: There are two types of 'character' shots. The character can be a fellow holiday maker, or a local. The fellow holiday maker is a special example of the 'new social group' where an individual is picked out. This may be a way of indicating our indebtedness to them for their entertaining, supportive or informative conduct; it may be an acknowledgment of sexual attraction (or liaison) or just a way of pulling an interesting-looking person into our group.

The local 'character' is another anthropologically inspired image [see p. 49]. Some find it hard to take these photos. They are aware that their response to the locals is shallow and based upon stereotyping. The cheeky youth, the knowing stallholder, a weatherbeaten peasant: the contact required to request a pose is difficult to achieve; ideally it should be 'real' contact, outside of the falsity of touristic relations. Ideally, the subject should give us their 'magical specialness' on the photo. It is probably for this reason that the most common 'local character' appearing in our albums is the tour guide, the lifeguard or the gardener. They are unlikely to cause embarrassment by refusal.

Outings: These are musts for photographs, they are the mobile equivalent of tourist sites [see p. 53] and they also fulfil the social group requirements: gathering together the members of our party for a shared experience. On these trips, the other major sorts of holiday photo are compressed into a short period of heightened 'holiday time'.

Travelling often takes up most of the time, and because we assume that photos through the window of our vehicle will not be worth taking, we arrive at our stopping points dying to relieve ourselves, both physically and psychologically. All that magical, different scenery was denied us on our journey. The experience of being 'away' has no record for us to share (and enhance) in later picture viewing sessions at home. So we take pictures at these stops, regardless of their suitability, or the presence of (and our purchase of) impressive postcards costing less than a photo.

The intinerary of such outings, where quantity of sights replaces quality of seeing, only allows for very short stops at many of the points of interest. This is what creates the familiar spectacle of 45 people tumbling off a coach, taking similar photos, going to the toilet and then milling about. Ten minutes is all the itinerary allows,

'Hey, stop, that's where J.R. Lives':
Outings themselves may be arranged to
go to sites that are only sensible in
reference to completely fictional events.
See 'Outings' and 'Sites'.

Holiday fooling: Compare this image of
holiday fooling with p. 41. Both were
taken on the same holiday, showing how
larking about is infectious in form as well
as in general.

long enough to 'stretch one's legs' and take a snap but not long enough for anything else. The tour guides are up against the hidden pressures of arriving at sites before 100 other coaches, or getting to eating houses which give them free meals for bringing custom. So they may even tell tourists where to go and what to take for 'good pictures' within the limited time available.

Sites: By these I mean special sites for 'attractions'. Not the 'new landscape', 'new buildings' or 'local activities' but those views, activities and institutions presented to us as 'essential' tourist experiences. Dean MacCannel in his book *The Tourist*[30] explicates an underlying rationale to such situations. His book was written prior to the mushrooming of package holidays and is less relevant to these 'costa' resort holidays than the tour, which he approaches as an activity defined by the middle-classes in the Edwardian period. Still, his ideas are provocative. He understands anything to be a potential attraction (what he calls a 'sight'). It merely requires us to be told that a particular thing is an attraction. (Preferably prior to arrival at the site of the attraction, and with some appeal to cultural history or exposed cultural veracity.) All that remains is for us to recognize the attraction at the site, and its function as 'sight'/site is established.

Photographs of the 'sight'/site are part of the circulation of information which gives us prior warning that an experience *is* an attraction. We take our own photos to prove our dutiful attendance and

Sight/site: This photo shows a street intersection in Dallas. Or rather, it shows *the* street intersection where President Kennedy was shot. The book depository and surrounding area are one of the strongest sight/sites in the modern world, spread as it was through the global village by the burgeoning mass media.

enable us to recite our knowledge of the attraction when back home. Of course, we take them partly because we expect that others will appreciate having at least this second-hand experience of sight-seeing. After all, we were willing to pay for the sight, having been convinced of its importance by the prior images and information proclaiming its importance.

The albums, part four: weddings

Proof positives: These are another must for vernacular photography. The history of weddings' photographic records is generally recognized to consist of a shift from formal professional documents towards informal amateur snaps.[31] However, the official record is

The happy couple: A suitably authoritative picture of the couple's second marriage. Second marriages, even when occurring much younger than this (as most do) seldom have the same density of photographic coverage as the first time around.

The wedding photo: See text.

still entrusted to the professional. This minimizes the risk of leaving no suitably probative and authorative version of this important rite of passage. Such professional photos can be included in the vernacular field. Collectively we have stipulated their generic forms and we put them in our albums to use them as we do our own vernacular photos. Wedding snaps tend to duplicate the professionals' or to follow the rationales already laid out for family and special occasion photos [see pp. 25–45]. The following are the sub-species of wedding photo which have not been dealt with in the previous discussions.

Exit from the church: This series of photos comprises the archetypal wedding shots and is still entrusted to professionals. A certain structure is maintained. One photo will depict the bride and groom, another the couple and their parents; a third will record them and the bride's family and the fourth, the couple and the groom's. There may be others, but these are the basics. These stereotyped images may be questioned by the young couple but the professional will recommend them as necessary. This is not just because the depiction of all those in attendance will guarantee maximum reprints (the most profitable aspect of wedding photography), but because the experienced photographer knows that the couple are not autonomous when it comes to the post-wedding assessment of the photographic record. Uncle George and great aunt Georgina may have strong assumptions about what wedding photos should depict and their position in the family may enable them to taint the family memory of the event by broadcasting their disappointment with the record.

Such photos are required to depict the ties that constitute family and tribal lineage. Marriage is an event whose meaning at one level is structured by these family relations. In the 'exit from the church' photos this structure is most evident.

These ties are very important. The sociologist Pierre Bourdieu saw this use of photography as emblematic for vernacular photography. He called it photography's 'integration' function.[32] Whilst photography is used for much more than this nowadays, it remains a fundamental aspect of vernacular photography.

Signing the register: the ultimate probative vernacular photo. It is a fairly recent phenomenon because of technical and ethical problems. This sacred/legislative act must be revered, and the impersonal and commercial presence of the photographer (with accompanying disruptive activities) was only recently outweighed by market forces. In its formal structure (of the couple combined in the act of signing) the photo echoes the longer-lived image of cake-cutting.

The cake: Cutting the cake has long been the other symbol of marriage. Here the couple join hands in a secular display of joint effort aimed at symbolically distributing the fruits (fruit cake) of successful family provision. The ritual's secularity has enabled it to be a photographable moment for longer than signing the register. In the general festivities of the wedding reception, flash photography

The cake: See text.

(originally an explosive event!) and photogenic rearrangement can be taken on board easily. Indeed, such 'sealing' of the ritual's importance may contribute to the atmosphere.

Codicil

Funerals: This is the other major event which requires attendance by the extended family. In the late twentieth century it doesn't feature in collections of vernacular photography. Whilst the family structure is as evident at these events as at weddings, death changes the situation considerably. Rather than celebrating the enlargement and success of the family (almost a tribal acquisition) a funeral marks the reduction and impoverishment of the group.

People do photograph their dead loved ones[33] but they keep them private and do not include the mourners. Such a talisman of the

The respected dead: Trade union funerals, armed forces and other organizations with strong hierarchies do generate funeral photos. Along with respect for the dead, these photos can prove a person's loyalty and commitment which can help in promotion, but also, when the wind changes, they can be used against them.

dead can be a powerful aid to mourning and the management of grief.

Exceptions to the above may occur if the deceased has risen to prominence in the community. Their growth in social status can be celebrated. The likelihood of vernacular photography (as opposed to professional, news-generated 'obituary photos') is increased if the extended family group is widely dispersed, or mainly centred far away. In these circumstances the probative nature of photography may be important. A branch of the family can prove their proper treatment of the dead by circulating images showing the favoured family trappings. This proves their success as a family. Throughout the period between photography's inception and the Second World War, emigration and its uncertainties resulted in many such photos.

Prior to the First World War, the death of young children was as regular in the West as it is now in the so-called developing nations. The gynaecological risks of motherhood were greater and this put a high premium on children's survival. Photo historians have noted the relative ubiquity of child corpse photographs which allowed the facts of death to be negotiated by portrayal as 'still life' or 'sleep'.[34]

The albums, part five: environmental

Our environment: It is difficult to categorize exhaustively vernacular photographs because they are seldom simply of one subject, the holiday group is also a landscape, the family portrait is also a picture of possessions. The image usually portrays the physical context of the event photographed. This physical context to our lives is important. It holds connotations that go beyond the environment's ostensible meanings. We have already looked at houses, cars and views in this way [see pp. 31–2] but our neighbourhood, town or region can all produce subjects personally meaningful enough to demand photographing.

Aesthetic considerations can play a part in such photography. Keen amateurs may be largely motivated by their perception of the aesthetic qualities held by their environment. Other vernacular

A photo can make anything beautiful:
With so much damage being done to our
environment, it is an open question
whether documenting it in an aesthetic
manner pricks our consciences and
makes the images stay with us.
Unfortunately, pollution is not mainly an
individual problem, but one engendered
by macro-economics.

photographers, whilst not blind to the picturesque, may be more motivated by stories attached to places and areas. Keen amateurs will fasten on details and abstract out images that stand as metaphors for wider concerns and attitudes. Light on decrepit concrete, broken windows, sun reflected from buildings, reflections in puddles, can all become beautiful metaphors of urban existence. But the most frequent environmental picture is that which constitutes a 'landscape' photo.

Landscape: A prerequisite of most holidays or outings is to 'go somewhere different' to differentiate our leisure activity from the everyday. Most people in the photographing nations live in towns or cities, and the big symbol of difference to town is country; to building is tree, to road is stream and so on. The landscape photo is the sign of difference to urban existence. The development of this bipolar opposition has a history, it is neither natural nor arbitrary, but historically and culturally inflected.[35] Because vernacular photography concentrates on the exceptions to routine and leisure rather than work, most photos are taken in such 'country' (though this may be the country of cities, i.e. parks).[36] In the past this was compounded by technical considerations that favoured the extra light available outdoors. Nowadays these no longer apply, but landscapes still dominate.

The popular aesthetics of landscape are still a mixture of Classical and Romantic painting which distilled into photo-pictorialism around the first quarter of the century.[37] This harbours interesting

The romantic landscape: See 'Landscape'.

contradictions at its roots. The Classical tradition draws from the pastoral idealization of land as a potential Arcadia, satiating man's needs and wants. The Romantic celebrates our exciting vulnerability before an awesome landscape which demonstrates the magnificence of its creator Dame Nature.[38]

What is common to such representations of landscape is an attitude in which seeing (depicting) is a privileged and coherent act, if not of mastery, then of a secure, detached but interested observer. The patchwork fields stretch out *below* us (somewhat reminiscent of a map given to the new squire on accession to the estate), the mighty waterfall crashes in front of the lone onlooker (to give scale) whilst we, the observer, look on from a discreet distance. This psychological position of privileged seeing dovetails well with photography's linear perspective (where all points refer back to the viewer through the inversion of the vanishing point),[39] its ability to record fine detail, and the capture of all that information at the touch of a button!

The most important thing about landscape for modern man is that it is the most widely recognized sign of nature. However implausible this may actually be in the industrialized nations, landscape is taken to be natural.

Nature: If we include domestic pets and flowers as examples of nature, then this category (which subsumes landscape) is probably the largest in western nations' vernacular photography.

Nature as metaphor: We often use nature to say something about ourselves. Here a felled log has been worn away by people climbing over it. The light emphasizes its skin-like surface, as its branch echoes a limb. The dead pseudo-body is walked over by those eager to take a short cut through the woods.

Most people's experience is that of the urbanite. Nature is felt to be that which contrasts with everyday experience. The popularity of nature programmes on TV testifies to the potential fascination of this 'anti-culture'. TV narrativises other living things' existence and turns the whole ecosphere into a vast collection of potential metaphors for human experience. The complexities of existence can be simplified and played back in the guise of 'natural history'. This use of information about nature has a much longer history than that of the electronic media. Certainly it has been a factor throughout photography's existence. This combination of nature as difference and also as metaphor, invades our picturing of nature.

Trees: Not only do trees crop up throughout our photos because of their genuine ubiquity, they are also a frequent subject in their own right. Trees can be impressive, with connotations of natural strength, stoicism and yet abundant life. On their own these attributes are somewhat too abstract to demand photographing in the vernacular mode, but trees also have interesting shapes and appeal to our abstract aesthetic sense. They also 'put us in our place' by defining nature's scale. (This is 'grand nature' in the tradition of Romanticism.)

The green of trees in leaf is a contributory factor too. Beyond plastics, paints and textiles, green is *the* natural colour[40], it's chlorophyll, 'the stuff of life'. Urbanites know, even if subconsciously, that the true opposite of their grey-black-brown-ochre world is green, whatever colour theorists might say!

Trees appear also as contorted, thwarted abstract shapes. Between Autumn and Spring, trees show off their skeletal structure and this is another subject for vernacular photos. The twists and turns of roots and branches display the marvelous complexity of nature. Cloudless skies at this time of year give a rounded limb-like quality to trees appendages so that their metaphoric value for humanity is strong. The gash left by a fallen branch calls up associations with eyes or mouths. Walt Disney exploited this anthropomorphism when animating trees in his early movies.

Strong prevailing winds, or other adversities make their presence clear in trees. The tree which is curved against the wind, or precariously rooted in rock, call our attention as they provide fantastic shapes and illustrate the power of growth to win through. The tree is an important icon of popular pantheism.

Animals: Wild animals hardly figure in photo albums. The patience, skill and equipment necessary to photograph indigenous species take such photographs out of the vernacular arena.

Most animal photos are of pets [see p. 40] but we do photograph domesticated livestock and zoo or wildlife park animals. We photograph these in two main modes: (1) as potential pets, (2) as 'natural' beasts. The first mode entails relating to the animals as potential mirrors of aspects of ourselves. The lamb skips for joy, the cow is inquisitive, the bear is bored. Some animals (usually with the big eyes and rounded contours reminiscent of a human infant[41] are considered 'cute' and our nurturing/possessive instincts are brought into play – we take them home as 'pet photos'.

Animals: Children and animals are a popular subject.

The second mode celebrates animals' otherness, their strength and unpredictability, which at least to a degree, constitutes a threat. Such as it is, this threat is substantially ours. Our repressed desires, fears and unpredictabilities are displaced onto the 'wild' creature. By photography, we capture the threat and symbolically control it. Nature is denatured.

Another aspect of animals' otherness is the opposite of strength: vulnerability. The shy (i.e. human-avoiding), delicate or rare animal is captured on film to prove its special faith in us, we who have got close enough to take a snap – with a transparent aura of fellow feeling acting as our flag of truce.

Water: This features in our 'natural snaps' too. Like landscape, for most of us it is different from our everyday environment.

Water tends to be photographed in one of four different modes: firstly, as an element of calm, the lake reflecting the surrounding hills and sky. Secondly the opposite, the romantic gush of the waterfall, the torrent of the mountain stream. Thirdly, streams as metaphors: of cleaness, freshness, innocence, even life itself. Images often draw upon these metaphors severally, as a complex nexus. In this mode we have our loved ones pose close to the flow, to make a symbolic connection. Lastly, we photograph water in connection with activities such as sailing. Here the appearance of water may be subordinate to the celebration of our power to act in the environment.

Details: I have already mentioned the preference for photographing details which may act as metaphors for larger concerns, or call to mind the complexities of nature and even stand in for the human form. There is another motive behind many detail shots: inquisitiveness and the desire to understand. Moving in close and 'looking hard' (at least, hard enough to take a photo) can reveal new levels of information which are pleasurable to encounter. TV nature documentaries play on this close-up revelation, which, combined with an increased density of information on the commentary, can feed back

Details: Apparently this was an attempt to photograph a beautiful caterpillar. Unfortunately, many of our cameras can't help us in our desire to know, because they can't focus close enough.

on itself to enhance the feeling of revelation possible in 'looking hard'. By a reverse of the perspective of a photo [see p. 59 and note 37], we can lionize ourselves for being interested or thoughtful enough to 'see' this detail. Of course, merely looking is not understanding and often our lack of scientific knowledge is also raised as an issue by our detail photos. As is frequently the case, our experience is mixed. We both celebrate our interest, confront our ignorance and attempt to learn more.

Flowers: In the UK, gardening is the second most popular 'leisure time' activity after shopping.[43] Even those without a garden often have house plants to test their 'green fingers' on. Therefore it is not surprising that we take pictures of our flowers. However, only competitive gardeners often take pictures of vegetables. Flowers' colour and fineness, their precise regular form, combined with the visible sign of success in gardening care they manifest, make them a must for photography. This is obviously more pronounced with colour film's ability to record their hues, but even in black-and-white flowers have been a significant subject for photography. Importantly, they are usually cut flowers, the wedding/anniversary/birthday bouquet, and so perhaps are better considered as emblems of rites of passage [see p. 28]. In black-and-white, the subject is usually something like a single coloured rose bush planted on a special day or the physical layout of a garden, subjects which constitute a creative labour in itself.

There is more time to devote to gardening when children are grown up. This period coincides with an increased likelihood of taking up photography as a hobby. Manufacturers are currently trying to put the two together with camera kits and workshops aimed at mature people photographing flowers. The kits contain close-up lenses and the workshops are specifically aimed at older people.[44]

Summary: Usually we consider the act of snapping our day-to-day lives as inconsequential fun, but it can be usefully regarded as much more than that. This consideration of the general image categories which appear in photo albums has thrown up many complex interconnections between this apparently private sphere and wider society.

Still, when all is said and done, we take photographs because it is pleasurable. It is a way of marking life's experiences as valuable and responding more-or-less enthusiastically. This fundamental facet of vernacular photography is a dependable human trait, and a whole industry is built upon it. One aspect of that industry is the photographic press, which relates to our domestic desires in a similar way to the lifestyle press of women's magazines and the home decoration monthlies. In the next chapter we will take a look at this specialized field of publishing, which is important for its construction of the 'serious amateur' market as opposed to the vernacular [see pp. 89–92].

3 Photographic magazines

Where do we get our ideas about what amateur photography is, or should be? A lot of them are picked up in the family. At first we are the subject of adults' photographs and learn what it is to be photographed. Along with this comes the experience of having our shared lives partially reflected back to us through such photos. Even when we, or our nearest and dearest, are absent from the image, as in views and 'interesting details', these images are judged by their relative importance for us and our family. Essentially, a good vernacular photo is one that is meaningful within that special world of knowing shared by us and those closest to us.

When we take photos ourselves we strive to produce these tokens of shared meaning, and learn that such things as 'getting it all in', 'getting close enough', 'having enough light', 'holding it steady', and so on are all important in making the desired image effective.

On top of all this, the media present us with models of what constitutes a good picture and, in the case of the photographic press, what constitutes amateur practice. Certainly, far more people take photos than read such magazines, but thousands do read them. Indeed, for people beginning to make photography into a major leisure pursuit, these magazines are often the main resource for the hobby's development. To judge by the ever increasing size of the photographic market (and the expensive hardware end of it in particular), these 'serious amateurs' are now more numerous than ever before.

One of these magazines, *The Amateur Photographer* [AP] is a longstanding publication, widely used by the British photographic retail trade as a benchmark, and available throughout the English speaking world. The AP can be used as a representative example of the photographic press, to see how the magazines depict photography to its readers.

General analysis of content

The first thing to note is that the AP is a weekly magazine. This is rare in photographic publications. All the other well-known ones worldwide are monthlies. Although each issue has a cheaper cover price than its monthly rivals, its cost per month is about three times that of the others. It might be surmised that this should effect the make-up of its consumer group, but its pitch is so similar to the other magazines that this seems not to be the case. With a circulation of some 75,000, it would seem that those interested enough in photography to buy magazines on the subject can afford the extra expense.

The increased costs of producing a weekly (all other things being equal) would lead us to expect more advertising. However, the other magazines follow the AP's format strikingly. Even American publications, such as *Popular Photography*[1] echo the format. The AP would seem to maintain its position by virtue of its cheaper paper and its greater circulation.

Advertising space

These magazines have a lot of advertising in them, between 50 and 60 per cent of the content. About half of this is in the form of glossy large or full page advertisements. This sort of percentage is not typical of other hobby magazines. *Cycling Weekly*, another magazine from the same publisher, has about half the advertising. The photo press (like the audio and computer press) has a level comparable to the monthly lifestyle magazines such as *Harpers And Queen* and *Cosmopolitan*, rather than other weeklies. By virtue of volume alone, the ads in the AP (and by extension, other photo magazines) are obviously an important part of the whole message of the magazine; they seem to say that amateur photography is about consuming. (This point will be discussed later [see p. 66].)

There is an apparent exception to this general rule. A format exists which has only about half the usual percentage of advertising. (The American title *Photo-Graphic* is one of these.[2]) However, the articles are suffused with product information and prices, often to the point of being advertising features in all but name. So the general contention about magazines' formats remains: they signal a consumption orientation.

The question may be asked: 'Is this prevalence of advertising a new phenomenon, linked to the growth of popular consumerism?' Looking at the AP of the 1930s reveals a strikingly similar advertising ratio. This may be related to the fact that the 1930s saw the first wave of consumerism for the lower-middle classes and photography was a considerable feature of it. Pre-war APs will be used for historical comparison throughout this chapter.

Editorial content

The AP shows a high degree of consistency in its editorial content. It begins with 'News' and then information on competitions, exhibitions and meetings. Following this are letters and readers' questions.

The majority of the features interspersed between these regulars are two- or three-page articles with display photographs. They are on photographic equipment, techniques and subject matter. The magazine's non-advertising content always finishes with a review of equipment and prices – the 'Buyers' Guide'.

Comparison with the pre Second World War AP shows great similarities of content distribution. Whilst the magazine was only one third of its current size, all the topics covered in the 1990s were evident in some form in the 1930s.

Currently, the majority of the feature articles fall into four categories: 1) Consumer information; 2) Photographic techniques; 3) Individuals' working methods and their results; 4) Making money from photography.

1. Consumer information

Interestingly, looking at the four pages of news per week, it emerges that the vast majority of information is about products and services. Combining this with the equipment information/consumer reports, it can be seen that about 25 per cent of the editorial pages are devoted to presenting photography as an arena of meaningful consumption. When this is combined with its advertising, and the 'Buyers' Guide', 65–75 per cent of the magazine is devoted to selling the idea of photography as consumption.

One of the other main areas of content, 'photographic techniques', also strays into this area. The readers' questions, overwhelmingly concerned with technical problems, are often about questions of what to buy to put things right. The articles on technique are often features encouraging the use of extra equipment, which is on sale elsewhere in the magazine. Altogether, the AP's loudest claim to your attention can be summed up in one word, 'BUY!'.

2. Photographic techniques

Concerns with technique feature every week. As well as the specific articles contributing about ten per cent of the content, the majority of correspondence, and numerous references in the individuals' portfolio features relate to this area. Not surprisingly, this is an important area of the magazine's preoccupations. Techniques are often linked to a concern with technology, which frequently comes back to equipment and purchase.

3. Individuals' working methods.

The AP's concern with individuals' working methods and their results is particularly interesting. (These articles have their direct precursors in the thirties 'How I Make My Exhibition Pictures' features.[3]) Whilst suffused with information on techniques employed and equipment owned, the really striking thing about these photographers is that the vast majority are professionals. Their approaches are professional and their assumptions as to what makes a good picture are professional. Their unspoken guide to excellence is the market place. 'What sells?' is the watch-word for their aesthetic.

Even those amateurs who do make the feature pages are ingrained by this approach. Most of them are semi-professionals, and their goals are framed by the professional market. Even these 'amateur' photos comprise only something less than 5 per cent of the magazine's photographic content. (In fact the largest category of photographs, discounting the adverts, is the 'product shot'!)

As we shall see, the professionalization of these amateurs is completed by the dominant tenor of the amateur photographic press.

4. Subsidizing your hobby

The blurred distinction between the AP's 'successful amateur' and the professional photographer is echoed in the prevalence of articles and smaller statements that specifically address the issue of making money from photography. Since the invention of photography, photographers have been concerned with getting some return on their outlay. It has always been an expensive business, and although becoming cheaper and cheaper, the 'serious amateur' is committed to great expenditure. (Not least by the general 'BUY!' approach of photo magazines.) The AP of the 1930s has a similar undercurrent, evidenced by regular letters on the subject.

However, in today's market-orientated popular photography, where success is measured in terms of sales, the relationship is not purely one of subsidy. It is assumed that a photo, if good, will be saleable and, if saleable, it is good. Previously, adherence to a rigid pictorialist code of aesthetics, or the employment of modernist 'essentially photographic' approaches were applauded and given exhibition prizes – which used to be the main recognition of success. Today competitions are often just marketing ploys and success is measured in terms of suitability for publication.

This yardstick by which readers of the photographic press are encouraged to measure themselves (for it is a feature of all the large

AP/FUJI 1991 CALENDAR

THE FOUR SEASONS

Have your picture published in the AP/Fuji 1991 calendar and win a share of £3000!

SPRING

SUMMER

AUTUMN

WINTER

E veryone uses a calendar and every amateur photographer wishes he or she could have one of their photographs hanging on the wall depicting a month on a calendar.

Well, here is your chance. *AP* and Fuji have combined to organise a photographic competition whereby you stand to win some lovely lolly as well as have the thrill of seeing one of your photos featured in next year's calendar to be given away free with the last issue of *AP* for 1990.

We have £3000 in prize money to give away!

How to enter

The theme for the competition is **The Four Seasons.** The winter and spring sections have passed so *AP* and Fuji are looking for photographs which depict the British summer. We will be picking the three summer pictures to illustrate the summer months on the calendar. The best picture of these three will win the photographer £250 while the two runners-up each receive £125. This method of awarding prizes will also apply to autumn entries.

All photographs must be taken on Fuji film. Only one photograph per entry is allowed. Entries can be colour or black and white prints (no bigger than 12x8in) or slides.

Closing date for summer entries is August 24.

The three winning pictures will be published in *AP* September 22 issue, when we will also announce the closing date for the autumn competition's entries.

The photo that the judges find to be the best of the 12 calendar images will win the photographer £1000!

So get out among the hills and beaches and show us the beauty of the British summer. And don't forget to load your camera with Fuji film. ∎

RULES

1. This competition is open to bona fide amateur photographers only, ie those who do not make their living as a photographer.
2. Entrants must submit one photograph only, taken on Fuji film. Black, white, colour prints and slides are acceptable. The photograph must be taken by the entrant. Do not mount prints.
3. A stamped, self-addressed envelope must be provided if entries are to be returned. Do not send loose stamps, postal orders or cheques.
4. All entries must be clearly identified and complete with technical information.
5. Copyright of the entry remains with the photographer. Any non-prizewinning shot used will receive the standard reproduction fee. Also prizewinning shots can be used as part of a promotional campaign.
6. While every care will be taken of the entries while in the possession of the organisers, we cannot be held responsible for any loss or damage. Entrants enter at their own risk. Proof of postage will not be accepted as proof of receipt.
7. The prizes will be as stated and cannot be exchanged.
8. The judges' decision is final and no correspondence can be entered into.
9. Employees of Reed Business Publishing or Fuji Photo Film (UK) Ltd and their families are ineligible for entry.
10. Closing date for the summer competition entry is Friday, August 24. No entries will be accepted after this date.
11. Entries to be sent to AP/Fuji 1991 Calendar competition, *Amateur Photographer,* Prospect House, 9-13 Ewell Road, Cheam, Surrey, SM1 4QQ.

Success! – The transformation to commodity.

circulation photographic magazines) necessarily leaves some things out of the account. Primarily it puts personal meaningfulness outside the 'frame'. This facet of vernacular photography is axiomatic for most of us as we begin photography. The problem starts when, in order to make more meaningful images, we take on board the necessity to improve our techniques, begin to read the magazines, and are subtly immersed in a new area of personal meaning. Thus, we are alienated from the source of our photographic impetus. Additionally, building up skill takes time, and the experimentation necessary can work against our spontaneous involvement in (and the recording of) the events we initially wished to record.

Cynically, it might seem that the photo press takes a largely healthy social phenomenon, ('vernacular photography') and steers it into the market place for its imaginary satisfaction through buying consumer goods. This keeps the market buoyant, which produces advertising, the revenue of which keeps the magazines going.

A change of analysis

In the discussion so far, attention has been given to the similarities in content between the 1930s AP and current editions. The earlier volumes' inclusion of examples of all the categories described above, and their similar percentage of advertising has been stressed. (This is a simple form of 'content analysis'.) A more complete analysis could address the magazines' devotion of a much smaller editorial space to consumption, and the much greater frequency of amateur photographs throughout. Both would indicate interesting areas of change. However, such comparisons of old and new, based as they are on percentage content figures and frequency of occurrence, can never prepare us for how different the two periods of the magazine feel when read in detail. 'Content analysis' is very good for getting to know an area of investigation quickly, and for mapping out consistent areas, but it may leave whole fields of meaning out of account.

Today's AP is a very professional product, businesslike and market oriented. In contrast, the 1930s AP is very much an enthusiast's journal, idiosyncratic, domestic, amateur. If the 1930s AP resembles a private journal, then the 1990s AP calls to mind a company prospectus.

Since the 1950s a favoured approach to assessing meaning has been 'structural analysis'. This relates elements to each other, seeking out meaningful absences and looks for opposing elements. In this way it attempts to go beneath the surface of manifest meaning and to place the elements in an overall structure of meaning. However, this is a detailed and dense procedure and in practice particular areas of a communication are usually selected for such treatment. Content analysis is useful as a way of selecting these areas and quantifying the more qualitative approach. The two methods can be used together. For example, content analysis has indicated that the promotion of consumption is a feature of the photo-press. An article could be chosen from one of the content analysis categories (say that on technique), and submitted ot structural analysis to see how it weaves consumerism into its structure of meaning.

Representation of women

Far fewer women appeared in the AP in the 1930s than do today. This is the sort of macro-feature which content analysis alerts us to and indicates a potentially interesting area for further analysis.

The way women are presented in the photo press gives us examples of how we might relate photographically to female models. Where these examples come from, whether they simply reflect photo practice, or construct it, may be revealed by an analysis that looks at the changes and developments in this area over a period of time [see p. 86]. This historical approach is not often attempted within a stucturalist analysis, but it is not by any means contrary to the spirit of it. I will start in the 1930s and move up to the present day.

Structural analysis

All cultural products can be treated as 'texts' for purposes of analysis. When approaching such 'texts' it is usual to start by looking at what is said and comparing that to what might be a contrasting statement. Sometimes these contrasts are present in the object analysed (i.e. examples are given), but more often, they are implicit.

The obvious oppositions in the article, 'Making Better Snapshots' [opposite] are those relating to technique and what might be termed 'a suitable approach for the photographer'. However, with our interest focused on the place of women in the communication, what becomes apparent is the lack of reference throughout the article to the woman in the illustrations. This absence is a feature of the overwhelming majority of the examples where images of women appear in the 1930s AP.

Incidentally, the heavy presence of the masculine third person pronoun, which would be such an obtrusive point nowadays, should – if possible – be put to one side. Although it does serve to emphasize *for us* the relative absence of the woman, in the thirties it was usual and indicative only of the wider society's trends, not photography's as such.

THE AMATEUR PHOTOGRAPHER & CINEMATOGRAPHER

August 25th, 1937

$\mathcal{M}$AKING BETTER SNAPSHOTS–12

By DAVID CHARLES.

This article is the twelfth of a series which is dealing, week by week, with matters of interest to the camera-user who is anxious to do full justice to his subjects.

Fig. 1. Action-pictures need as much care with regard to background as any others. This is typical of the hasty shot, or of the beginner's effort.

Fig. 2. By asking her to look round, the whole effect of concentration on the game is lost. A very usual beginner's mistake.

WHEN an attractive action subject such as that depicted here presents itself, it can be made into a very amusing competition among the camera owners present to see who gets the best results.

And such a competition usually turns out to be exceedingly instructive. It may not be the one who knows most about photography who wins. The person who has been used to taking his time over the selection of his viewpoint, the setting of the various adjustments of the camera, and careful, deliberate aiming is very liable to discover when he is at last ready to shoot that the tug-of-war is all over and the combatants have retired from the scene. The excitable person, on the other hand, will be all agog to get his shot in first. He will forget all about observation of the background, and is as likely to face the sun as not. Fig. 1, unless he has "beginner's luck," will represent the measure of his success.

The Expert's Failure.

But, most peculiarly, this

Fig. 3. Accidents will happen, and even the expert may find on development that he has caught an impossibly awkward pose.

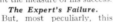

Fig. 3a. This enlargement of part of Fig. 3 shows even more clearly the awkwardness of the pose caught. Also it shows that movement was quite rapid, as the figure is nowhere sharp.

quite unpleasing outline is as likely to come from the camera of a more deliberate worker. It must be remembered that a certain amount of time elapses between the thought, "This is the picture I want," and the fall of the shutter on that scene. Part of that period is occupied with the actual exposure of course. But by far the greater part of the period is occupied

Fig. 4. "Taking the Strain" is a moment of comparative inactivity, giving time for a very rapid check of the desirability of the pose before shooting.

by the action of the brain in making its decision, in issuing its command to the fingers to shoot, in that message travelling down the arm to the fingers, in the fingers accepting the message and performing their function, and in the travel of the exposing lever before the actual exposure takes place.

Time-Lag.

That period is called "time-lag." With some shutters it is slightly longer than with others; with many people it is very much longer than with others. In most people the time-lag between observing the pic-

ture they want and release of the shutter is long enough to let both the girl and the dog entirely change their poses.

Be Prepared.

Even the most practised action-photographer, prepared to seize his opportunities in the instant they occur, is subject to the vagaries of fortune. He will not have winners every time, but his proportion of winners will be comparatively high. He is as liable as anyone else to find that a movement even swifter than his own has produced a result like Fig. 3, shown more clearly in the enlarged version of Fig. 3a; but if he is fond of curiosities he can always find a place for it in his album.

For the Deliberate Worker.

There are some who find that their mental and physical make-up fits them best for calmer activities than the rather hectic one of action-photography. And who will say that the picture of the peacemaking gift, after the war was over, has not as good a title to be considered for the prize as even Fig. 4, the best of the action shots?

Fig. 5. But the peacemaking after the mimic fight is still easier to photograph, and even the expert snapshotter tends to concentrate on these stationary poses. The result is so much more certain.

Doing 'full justice' to your subjects in 1937.

'Full justice to his subjects'

However, there are only five references to the woman in the text. Three of these are not gendered:

A. 'an attractive action subject' [line 1]
B. 'the combatants' [line 19]
C. 'the figure' ['Fig. 3a' caption]

Of this triplet of references, A subsumes the woman to the event – she is only present in this reference by virtue of her activity. In B she is given the same importance as the dog, and in C she is merely illustrative of issues involved in photographic technique. Through-out the 1930s when women appear in the AP, they are usually used to illustrate points of photographic technique.

The fourth reference to the woman is in the caption to the article's 'figure 2'. This is interesting because we are told that when she turns around (thus becoming the subject of the picture) the 'action sub-ject' is lost. Therefore this is considered a mistake. Of course, it is only a mistake if the woman is to be subordinate to the activity, rather than its focus. It is difficult to imagine the subject being treated in the same way in today's magazines.

The last written reference to the woman is 'the girl' [line 2, final column]. This seems incongruous as the woman is certainly not a juvenile and may alert us to another aspect of women's occurrence in the 1930s AP. Wives and girlfriends take their place alongside children, pets and servants as illustrations of preferred photographic practices. There are two common denominators for this collection of subjects. Firstly, they were generally available to the amateur photographer of the 1930s. Secondly, they do not have much of a social position from which to refuse the requests of the photogra-pher. They are relatively powerless.

Women in 1930s advertisements

Although the vast majority of photographers were male, there had been since the Edwardian era an awareness in the industry of the potential for bringing women into photography to swell the market.[4] In the 1930s, those people who had jobs were doing relatively well, prices of essentials were low, and more women had paid jobs than ever before. This was a changing time for the rela-tionship between women and amateur photography.

Looking at the advert for the Purma camera [p. 74], we can see this overt appeal to women as photographers. Ignoring all the other messages which come from this advert, the current concentration on women and photography highlights certain interesting facets of the

THE AMATEUR PHOTOGRAPHER & CINEMATOGRAPHER

February 19, 1936

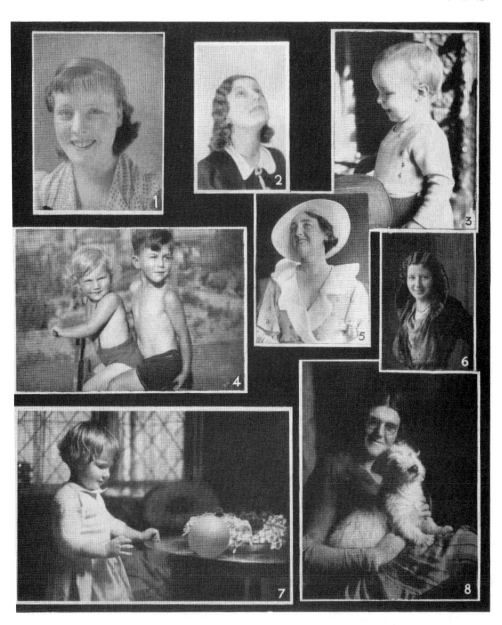

PRINTS FROM " THE 'A.P.' BEGINNERS' COMPETITION.

1.—" Daisy."
By William Patterson.

2.—" Adoration."
By E. W. Newton.

3.—" Alistair."
By Dr. J. A. Elliot.

4.—" Where are the Others ? "
By J. A. Holdcroft.

5.   " A Portrait."
By C. Newton.

6.—" Portrait of a Young Lady."
By Eunyn Eyles.

7.—" What Now ? "
By Noel Pearson.

8.—" Dinny."
By Irvine H. Green.

Reader's wives and other subjects.

June 24, 1936   *THE AMATEUR PHOTOGRAPHER ADVERTISEMENTS*   xix

A Miniature Speed Camera
with a
Focal-plane Shutter

No longer need you envy the man with an expensive camera, able to take any and every kind of 'speed' subject. Here is a camera at every man's price, equipped with the type of speed shutter which the Press photographer insists upon.

PURMA
PATENT ## SPEED CAMERA *for only*

Illustration shows the Purma Speed Camera, with ever-ready case, in action

Get a Purma Speed Camera to-day and take action pictures of diving, racing, birds in flight, children at play, and the numerous other subjects which you have often attempted with an ordinary camera and failed. Six instantaneous speeds, 1/25th to 1/200th sec. 16 pictures on 1/- vest-pocket roll film. No focussing necessary—everything from 6 ft. to infinity is sharply defined.

Never before has it been possible to enjoy speed photography at such little cost.

35/-
EVER-READY CASE 10/-

Look for the registered name *PURMA* on the ever-ready case.

The PURMA brings a new joy into travel and holiday picture-making. It opens up visions of subjects unobtainable in the ordinary way. Only too often does one see in murky streets and shaded surroundings pictures which experience tells you are not sufficiently well lit for successful snapping. But the PURMA will get them every time and your friends will say, "However did you take that one ? I couldn't have got it with my camera, in that light."

British Patent 430648 and 443907. World patents pending.

FROM YOUR PHOTO DEALER

Name of nearest stockist and illustrated prospectus from Sole Concessionaires :

R. F. HUNTER LTD
"CELFIX HOUSE," 51, GRAY'S INN ROAD, LONDON, W.C.1   Phone : Holborn 7311/2

'No need to envy the man': Women in the thirties did not have the economic position to form a market for the photo industry on their own.

advert's structure.

The first block of type next to the woman's right hand begins: 'No longer need you envy the man with an expensive camera, able to take any and every kind of "speed" subject'.

In conjuction with the image this surely aims most squarely at the woman who 'partners' a man committed to photography. However, to carry this line throughout would be to make the product into a 'woman's camera' and thus to limit its sales potential. To appeal to women *in addition* to men was to enlarge the market. Being associated with women *instead* of men was to be consigned to the small market of the few women economically active in the leisure sphere. (Although the number was growing, hence the advert.)

So, in the next sentence the advert attempts to have it both ways: 'Here is a camera at everyman's price, equipped with the type of speed shutter which the press photographer insists upon.' The rather visible hiatus between the two sentences can be related to the industry's problem of broadening photography's appeal to women. Since its inception, the medium had been so heavily gendered by a confluence of factors such as economics, scientism and social status that manufacturers had considerable resistance to overcome [see chapter one].

But this advert is still the exception. More often the place for women in the amateur photographic consumption pattern of the 1930s was as the (usually invisible) target audience for the man's photographic efforts. Or as the idealized 'little woman' who was the test of a camera's simplicity.

In summary then, the most frequent references to women in the 1930s AP are as 'Helpmate' (e.g., in the article analysed) or

Lightly sketched in: generally women played the role of appreciative audience to the keen amateur.

Women as mothers.

Beach mums.

'Mother'. Holidays may result in combining mother and seaside, but the modern representation as desirable object (characterized by the term 'pin up') is absent.

Infrequently (and very much seasonally) 'bathing beauties' do appear, but they are not depicted in the unreal manner we are so familiar with today [below]. The self-contained pose, the gummy grin and especially the mundane brassiere strap marks, make this

Beauty on the beach: More real woman, less object of desire.

Another tradition of looking: Woman as classical sculpture.

more a picture of a young woman than an offering of the object of desire.

In the art pages, where reproduction quality is generally better, there are infrequent studies of nude women. These draw upon ideals from fine art (not themselves neutral or timeless[5] and are references to classical sculpture and oil painting rather than simply the surrogate presence of an overtly sexualized body. They are illustrative of techniques deemed suitable at the time for the artistic rendering of photographic form and tone with the idealized (female) body.

Covering power

The covers of magazines are their most important messages. They present the whole magazine to the consumer and must make an impression which encourages purchasing. The content is trailed in ways calculated to engage the potential consumer's interest. So, they are constructed primarily to attract attention, be recognized by the regular buyer and generally signify 'Buy Me' from the top shelf.

The subjects of the thirties covers are almost entirely views and those categories familiar from the discussion of the models available [see p. 72] i.e., children, animals and mothers/women. Preponderant amongst these until the late forties were children and animals. From 1926 to 1967 the cover of the AP was an advert for a manufacturer or retailer. Many cover photos were the amateur prizewinners of the industry's competitions. By the late 1940s the balance of subject matter changed and images of women began to take over some of the children's cover spots as professional images began to replace competition winners.

In 1948, the first woman as 'young attractive woman', appeared on the cover [p. 78]. This heralded a steady increase in such images throughout the fifties and sixties. In 1954 full colour was introduced to the cover and in May 1955 the first colour 'cover girl' was published in an advert for Agfa film. Two years later Agfa again presented a 'pin up' whose *raison d'etre* was her attractiveness. Their sales pitch was that Agfacolor was adequate for the task of capturing the woman's beauty. This approach draws on the assumptions underpinning the classical art nude of the thirties. By this time young women's 'natural' attractiveness was being used as the test of the technology. This marks a decisive break from the thirties use of women to illustrate amateur photographic techniques.

By the early sixties half of the covers are 'cover girls' and the rest are the usual subjects. The 'pin up' image, which grew out of the 'bathing belle' still retained its seasonality, being more prevalent in the summer months. When the adverts that had brought us the

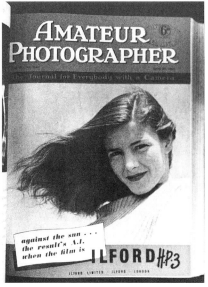

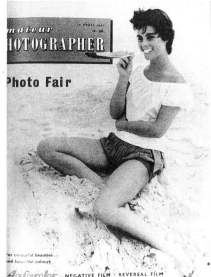

The cover girl is born.

The girl next door, or glamour girl?

cover girl disappeared from the cover, the desirable young woman stayed. By 1968 the cover girl was overwhelmingly the most usual cover image.

After a period of purposely titillating cover girls reached its peak in the late 1980s, (see pp. 80–84) 1990–91 saw a return of children, and animals. Pictures of women on the covers are now more diversified. This quick thumbnail sketch of the history of the cover girl in the AP is useful contextualization, but it doesn't give us much depth in comparison to our analysis of the 1937 article about beach photography [see p. 71 – not a bathing belle in sight there].

When a communication is almost entirely image based we need a specialized form of analysis. One of the most stimulating approaches is that used by Roland Barthes in the fifties and made famous in his analysis of a *Paris Match* cover in 1956–7.[6]

The cover's connotations

At the root of Barthes' approach is the disarmingly simple insight that an image is not the thing it pictures. This separation of the image from the thing allows the analyst to be clear about the levels of meaning being addressed. An example may make this clear.

In the cover of the AP of 6 April 1960 [right] the photo can, (at its most basic) be seen as a light patch covering most of the left half of the image, broken by some small light and dark areas. To the right is a large grey area broken by small light areas. We understand this tonal information to depict a man and a woman. This level of the image is known as 'denotation'. However, the image can be built on further when the denotation acts as a thing to another image.

In our case, the man and woman signify 'lovers'. This level of denotation plus a second process of meaning is known as 'connotation'. We know that they are lovers because we can read the signs:

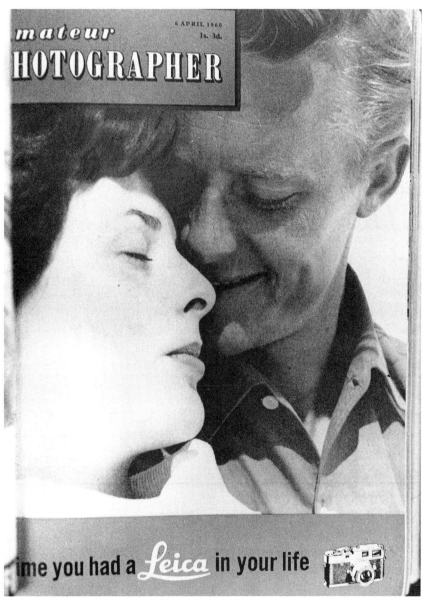

The family cover girl.

extreme closeness, ease of relating, the hint of a kiss, and of course – in the mass market – the heterosexual nature of the couple. This inventory of attributes, against which we can measure the denotation, can be thought of as a 'code'. This code fixes our reading of the connotation. For example, if the people were far apart, then the meaning would be in opposition to that of their closeness. This is because we are aware of the code of personal space by which separation indicates emotional distance. There are also other aspects of this 'spatial code' which are called up by this image. For example, the high/low opposition forms a code in which high (man) is dominant, and low (woman) is submissive.[7]

However, the process of meaning generation does not stop there because there are other connotations which are conjured up from our cultural knowledge in the context of 'Kissing Lovers'. These go something like this: sex – babies – family – the need to document your family growing up. This is the constellation of meanings that Leica draws upon in their caption 'It's time you had a Leica in your life.' The image and caption coalesce in the realm of meaning. Each favours metaphors in the other.

Uncovering the codes utilized by an image and understanding the various levels of meaning it contains is known as 'decoding' and can lead to surprising and valuable conclusions. So, we can see how the genre of the wife/helpmate image, so common in the thirties illustrations to articles on technique, has been changed. The wife/helpmate has been made sexy and desirable, but is still held within the idea of the family. Previously the photographic press's readership was assumed already to have a family and be middle-aged, because the sort of income necessary to become a keen photographer came with maturity. As wider economic forces enabled younger people to become the major leisure consumers, the pitch of the magazines changed to accommodate the fact. By the sixties, the assumption was that spare income was most likely to be experienced *prior* to parenthood.

The zenith of the cover girl

The 10 January 1968 cover is at once typical, and at the same time extraordinary. It is typical of the cover girl portrait which had become the staple cover image by this time, but its strength of message is extraordinary.

With visual communications such as this, we understand both the text and image concurrently. The denotative signs are a young woman, very near and slightly above our point-of-view. She is heavily made up. She has her mouth open and eyes closed, apparently in

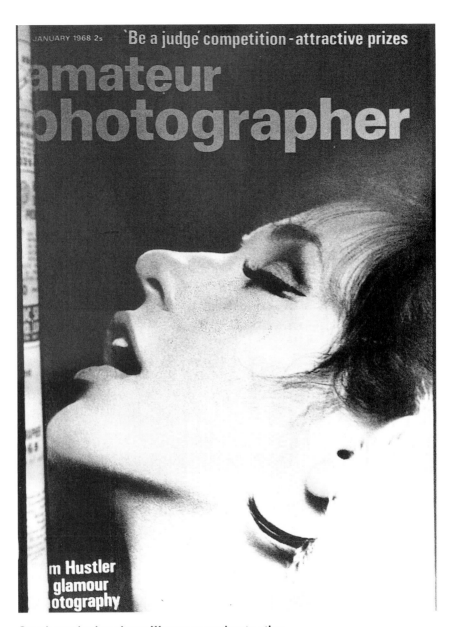

JANUARY 1968 2s   `Be a judge` competition - attractive prizes

amateur
photographer

m Hustler
glamour
otography

Overdetermined to please: Woman as passionate other.

ecstasy. This meaning is not fixed; she might be caught prior to a sneeze, or asleep and the photo turned through 90 degrees, (there are other possibilities, only limited by our imaginations). What contributes to our favouring the ecstasy reading is the text. It leads us to see this as an example of glamour photography, and to use our knowledge of how that represents women, to pick the most suitable

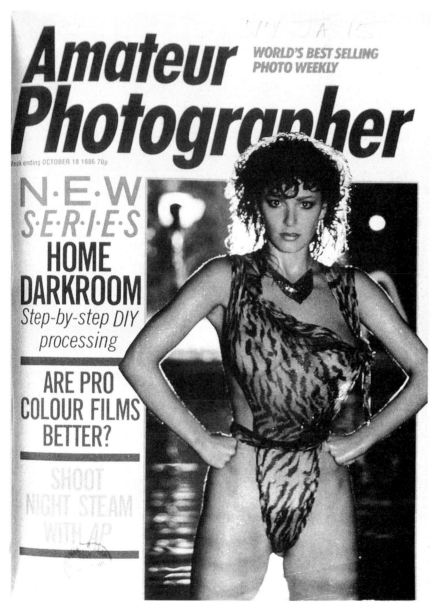

Woman as 'body': The bold emphasis of the torso, direct eye contact and wet lipped pout, all contrast with the 1930s circumspect pose and gummy grin [see p. 76].

meaning of the ambiguous image.

There is always room for other meanings in communication and it is the structure of the whole and its context which favours one of them over others. Text often serves to anchor a picture's meaning, as in the newspaper caption which tells us what a photo depicts.

Here the text is not a simple anchor but has a relationship known as 'overdetermination'. It tells us that the magazine contains an article on glamour photography. General knowledge of the photographic press and its young male target audience; of photographic conventions regarding suitable subjects for depiction; and the genre of the 'pin up', all combine with the text to determine the favoured interpretation.

Through the relationship by which a magazine's cover (no longer an advert for something else) is taken to be an advert for its contents, we are promised more revealing images, and more provocation of our desire, inside.

This sort of use of the cover girl was almost total in the mass photographic press by the 1980s. In 1986 all but two of the year's issues of AP had a cover girl. Generally, these are no longer portraits, but three-quarter length shots.

Many of the images, like the one here [left], re-work the old bathing beauty theme with swimming suits appearing in the most unlikely places (and the most unlikely garments getting wet!). In these three-quarter length pictures, the main denotative meaning is 'the body'. Contrast the pose of this model with the 1930s bather [see p. 76]. She is not represented in the guise of a challenge to film's tonal performance like the 1930s nude, and certainly not an illustration of technique or innovative practice. (In fact the image is unfocused.) Rather she is there as an unashamed 'come on' to the heterosexual male consumer. The whole layout is calculated to excite and give the impression of liveliness. The colours of the text in the original contrast with each other. The cover girl breaks out of her picture frame and 'over' the magazine's title.

Again, the main connotation is that of surrogate sexual excitement, with more to be had inside. That the address is so strident may perhaps be explained by increased competition in the leisure market. By the 1980s, there were many other photography magazines. Being monthlies, they sit on the shelves for longer. Making strident and obvious changes to the cover is one way for the publishers to try to separate out their weekly from the monthlies. But probably more important is the fact that hundreds of male leisure pursuit magazines appeared in the late seventies and eighties, for motorsport, hi fi, and so on. This produced a veritable Babel of visual cries shouting 'Buy Me' from the magazine racks.

The ambivalence apparent in the halting attempts of the thirties to appeal to women has been superseded [see p. 75]. The consumer power of women's leisure expenditure has never amounted to that of men, and the 'women's cash' which has emerged since the thirties has been attracted to fashion and cosmetics. (Hence the eighties attempt to engage young women in photography by marketing gaily coloured plastic compact cameras as fashion accessories.)

The photographic press does not concern itself with this segment of consumers, largely because it is directed at high-spending people, who are still overwhelmingly men. It is these whom the advertisers wish to contact. However, millions of compact cameras have been bought and used by women. If this results in just a percentage of these photographers becoming high expenditure consumers, then we may well see the sort of ambivalence of address noticed in the thirties returning in the nineties.

The use of sexy women on the covers had been well established in the photographic press for 20 years when the readers began to question the practice. Letters on the subject began to be published in the Spring of 1990. However, the photo press was initially unrepentant (possibly because the photographic market was showing no signs of anything but growth, whilst still being based squarely upon male leisure consumption). In reply to one letter the AP said:

> While it is indeed a positive thing that equality is becoming a reality in general life, there is no more reason for glamour to cease to exist as a branch of photography than for people to stop taking pictures of landscapes. Further, a visit to your local newsagent should impress upon you . . . that all UK photographic magazines have covers of approximately the same tone – as do, incidentally, many women's magazines [p. 14, 3.3.90].

In the Autumn George Hughes, then AP's editor-in-chief, endorsed the sentiments expressed in the Spring.[8] He was very concerned to defend the magazine from any accusations of cynically exploiting women in its use of cover girls. For him, glamour is simply another branch of photography, comparable to landscape or sport photography. As he says, the AP features the whole spectrum of amateur photography, and he intends it to carry on this breadth of coverage.

As mentioned earlier [see p. 78], the AP did in fact change its cover style in the last quarter of 1990 and toned down its cover girl images. In the first nine months of 1991, these comprised some 55 per cent of the covers. This turnabout was explicitly acknowledged by the editors.[9] Now, pin ups of a less provocative sort, faces echoing women's magazine covers and those illustrative of photographic techniques occur about equally.

On the inside

Although until recently the covers of photo magazines implied more of the cover's blatant titillation inside, they did not often deliver it. Generally the cover shouted what the content murmured. Whilst

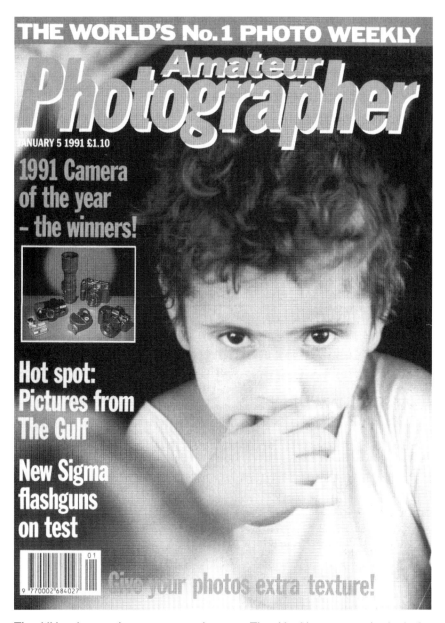

THE WORLD'S No. 1 PHOTO WEEKLY

Amateur Photographer

JANUARY 5 1991 £1.10

1991 Camera of the year – the winners!

Hot spot: Pictures from The Gulf

New Sigma flashguns on test

9 770002 684027

Give your photos extra texture!

The child makes a welcome return to the cover: The old subjects are coming back. As yet there does not seem to be a place for women as mothers.

glamour models are often used in the photo press to illustrate techniques in the places where the thirties AP would have used wives, children, pets or servants, it is only the glamour article (appearing every couple of months) which has the promised relation to the cover's message. As might be expected from George Hughes's position of 'broad coverage', despite the changes in covers, the frequency of glamour articles in the AP has remained roughly constant.

A return to the editorial content of the magazine would seem to be the surest way to see what message may come across to the purchaser concerning the place of women in amateur photography. In the non-glamour features, the images are still generally views, animals and children; with the addition of a large contingent of cameras and equipment (although there is a notable presence of sports photos). But whereas the women used to illustrate technical points in the thirties were amateurs, wives and girlfriends, today the women are professional (or aspirant) models. They are paid for what the thirties model could not refuse. So these models – purchased for multi-purpose photo sessions – frequently display the look of the cover girl, regardless of what illustrative purpose their image is pressed into later. In 1991 this use of images of woman was reduced by the AP. However, given the ease of acquiring such illustrations, it is an open question how long this will last.

Reflecting and constructing practice

In the thirties AP there was a strong do-it-yourself content, which consisted mainly of a constant flow of hints and descriptions of homemade gadgets, sent in by the amateurs themselves. So, combining this with the prevalence of amateur images it is obvious that the thirties AP does reflect at least some of what they did. At the same time, the prevalence of articles concerned with improving techniques demonstrates that constructing photographic practice was one of the purposes of the photo press (as it manifestly still is). However, the interchangeability of women, animals, and children, as illustrative subject matter – coupled with the lack of overt reference to any of these subjects – indicates that women were relatively peripheral to how amateur photography thought of itself in those days.

Current photographic publications do not contain a simple reflection of amateurs' practice because of the special ('professional') nature of those photographers and images published. That such magazines actively promoted an objectification of women cannot be doubted. This style of depicting women draws heavily upon an essential fact of public imagery. In at least the important sense of our *understanding* of the image, the *real* woman is not involved in the image. We must use codes of sexuality, body posture, dress, women's relation to men and so on to read the image. All these codes consist of socially constructed units of denotation and connotation too. There is never a real thing ('body') which the image gets us back to. In a world where so much of our knowledge and sensation comes from such sources, it is possible to argue that 'real' experience is swamped by this process of endless reference to codes.

The size of the market for large-breasted models, glamour studios, workshops and training videos, (all advertised each issue in the photo press) suggests that many readers must share these approaches to women as subjects for photography. What is still an open question is whether the attitude would exist at this level without the position taken by the magazines.

Future work

It would have been interesting to have moved on from this chapter to look at the 'serious amateurs' these magazines are aimed at, their clubs and the sorts of photographs they take. There has been some American work on this group but there is not room here to report it and respond with an analysis based on more recent British experience.[10]

4 Photography now

Markets

The size of the photographic market is huge. It has been estimated that the early nineties will see people in the UK take three billion photographs per year, in itself only a small fraction of the worldwide level of photography. (The USA reached this figure in 1974!) In 1987 £1 billion was spent on photography in the UK. What is more, this market is getting bigger at a faster rate than most other sectors of the economy. In Japan, for instance, this type of expenditure seems to be rising 50 per cent faster than general family expenditure.[1]

There are now so many cameras in use that only wristwatches outstrip them in the personal technology stakes. Something like 90 per cent of Britons over the age of 15 take photographs, and some 80 per cent of British households have two or more cameras. Given that many other countries have higher levels of vernacular photography, we can see the magnitude of the market.[2]

The photographic industry is not just large, it is also fully multinational. It manufactures its products wherever costs are cheapest. Political regimes or lack of skilled workers are no barriers to today's multinational corporations and modern assembly techniques.[3] For example, compact camera assembly is well established in South America; Japanese companies manufacture photographic equipment all over southeast Asia, including China, and it has been estimated that soon the Japanese Canon Corporation will not make any of their cameras in Japan.[4]

All this worldwide production is highly automated. Although it may be cheap in labour costs, its capitalization is expensive. If overall market growth is to be sufficient, the marketing wings of these companies not only need to keep established consumers buying their products, they must also find and expand new markets.

Going into the 1990s, the industry hitched itself to green issues, with manufacturers sponsoring conservation reports, and launching environmental photographic competitions. The photographic tradition of landscape pictorialism enables the industry to claim a special relationship with environmental concerns. In this way companies hope to ride the green consumer wave. I am not aware of photographers pressing manufacturers on these issues; they have grasped green-ness of their own volition.[5] [But see p. 96 and note 23.]

The need for new markets has been a consistent factor in the growth of the photographic industry. At the moment developing countries are used to off-load old, discounted technology so as to encourage them to get involved in photography and climb on the merry-go-round of photo consumption. Children are also offered yesterday's technology, repackaged as fun cameras, presented more-or-less as toys.[6]

Women are a consistently under-realized market [see pp. 72–5]. The male tradition of photography seems to have resulted in this group being a particularly difficult marketing proposition.[7]

Currently, demographic changes in the West mean that the elderly are a new growing leisure market with proportionately more potential expenditure than ever before [see p. 36]. It is no surprise that the photographic industry is beginning to woo them with specialist equipment and courses.[8]

While it is possible to be reasonably certain about the current size and continuing growth of the vernacular photographic market, it is less easy to be confident about finer details – market trends, for example. Photography is characterized by rapid introduction and withdrawal of products and marked swings in hardware popularity. This can make fools of even the most informed commentators: in 1979 the Economist Intelligence Unit (a professional group of economic analysts) predicted the demise of the 35mm compact, squeezed out by automatic SLRs and the 110 camera.[9] Actually the 1980s saw a boom in compact promotion and sales, which resulted in its becoming the most popular amateur camera throughout the western world [see p. 90].

In 1980, Don Slater[10] saw the industry as being divided into two sections, the mass photography market (snapshooting) and the rest. He pointed out that, in economic terms, the industry is not centred upon equipment. Film sales and processing acount for around three-quarters of photographic business. When he was writing, Kodak produced over 75 per cent of the film, chemicals and paper used in Britain, and the bulk of snap cameras.[11]

Slater argued that this put Kodak in a controlling market position, with an interest in selling more and more films. Because the majority of film buyers only bought one or two films per year, encouraging these uncommitted photographers to buy just one more film would enlarge the market enormously. No other group of photo-consumers would make as much difference. For this reason, Kodak aimed at these 'non-photographers' and continued to push their 'you press the button, we do the rest' approach.[12] Kodak's rationale was that this group were uncommitted because of lack of interest, money or time to devote to photography; profitability would be best affected if film could be sold to these people on their terms. So, for Slater, the imperative of maximizing film sales works against encouraging snapshooters to take their activities seriously.

Since Slater made this analysis, Kodak's near monopoly of mass photography has been severely undermined. Japanese film and camera manufacturers took away large amounts of their business. (Indeed, so much so that Kodak were forced to 'reorganize' well over 4000 employees out of a job in 1989.[13])

The Japanese made these inroads very much along the line of market development that Slater identified. They aimed at casual photographers by putting their film in supermarkets at point-of-sale positions, where impulse buying is greatest. Prices were cut (a big factor for low-volume film users), and the increased volume of processing kept developing and printing (D+P) prices down. They also introduced point-and-shoot 35mm compact cameras at prices much below Kodak's.

The end result was that the 'non-photographer' base of mass photography has been expanded, and not by one film purchase each per year, but by two or three. However, Fuji and Konica have benefitted most. So, the film market is much more diverse than it was in 1980.

With this new diversity, Kodak's approach seems to be changing. They have aimed at those amateurs who value results above price and kept their films relatively expensive, claiming technical superiority based upon brand name familiarity and extensive TV advertising. In this 'upmarket snaps' position, its interests are to encourage 'non-photographers' to become more committed and value the technical aspects of their results more. However, Kodak doesn't have it all their own way in this market niche, competition from Japanese manufacturers is fierce here too.

For Slater, the single-lens-reflex camera market exemplifies that section of photography left unexamined by his analysis of the market for uncommitted photographers. He associates this area of consumerism with techno-fetishism. It would seem to be this aspect of the wider market which has been picked up on in the move to make some 'non-photographers' more committed.

Being numerically small, the SLR market sector can be seen as needing constant turnover of cameras to keep sales buoyant. In a manner reminiscent of the car industry, where units are renewed every four years or so, SLR cameras are constantly traded in.[14] The motivating force behind this insistent renewal is the idea of constant technological revolution.

In this mythology electro-mechanical developments don't just make things happen better, they supposedly make previous technology redundant. As Slater says: '. . . the introduction of new technology is not meant to signify the entry of just another competing camera, but the replacement of all hitherto existing cameras.'[15]

Slater does not dwell on the process by which the sales imperative of product renewal is turned into a techno-fetishism on the part of the consumer, but the photographic press would seem to play a large part [see chapter three]. However, it can be easily seen how the techno-fetishistic desire for the most up-to-date, technology-laden equipment does dovetail with a small, high-value market requiring constant turnover. (Interestingly, this economic logic has created a large used camera trade, which again reflects the car market. This trade has mushroomed since Slater made his analysis.)

The techno-fetishism engendered in the SLR market (what Porter calls the 'serious amateur' market[16] has a facet which sees technological advance as reducing the skill necessary for a reasonable result. Using this rationale borrowed from the 'serious amateur' market, the 'upmarket' snapshooters are encouraged to take best advantage of their 'superior' film by using a 'superior' [auto-everything] compact camera. These are actually more expensive than many SLRs (especially secondhand ones).

So, rather than Slater's two-track amateur photographic market of the late 1970s, there seems to be at least a three-sector picture. Firstly, the 'non-committed', who are sold cheap and cheerful, hassle-free low expectation snapshooting. Secondly, the 'upmarket'

The bridge camera: Canon's Epoca camera has a built in 3X zoom lens with the features expected of an SLR, but you can't change the lens or see through it. It seems to have taken round edges to its ultimate conclusion.

snapshooters who put their faith in modern compact technology and high profile materials. Thirdly, the 'serious amateurs', who buy the newest super-duper techno SLR they can afford. This last group exhibit certain demographic characteristics, being aged 25 to 44 years and disproportionately male.[17] This is unsurprising, given the level of 'spare cash' necessary, and amount and type of leisure required. The male oriented nature of the amateur press probably contributes to this too.

This 'snapshot' of the photographic economy's social make-up is somewhat misleading. Its 'still image' leaves out of account the facts of personal development. People move from one category to another. Indeed, the industry has a notional 'ladder of consumption' by which a person starts as a non-photographer, moves up through the categories, and ends up as a semi-professional.[18] However, most people on the ladder move both up and down it. Women often move down when they have children, men when costs and failing health begin to bite.

A person is not 'just a snapshooter' by virtue of their innate faculties. Neither are they consigned to any category of practice for life. Too many commentators from George Eastman onwards have assumed that people are either one sort of photographer or another.[19] The fact that one's practice falls into one category *for the moment*, (and therefore more-or-less under its economic logic) has no bearing on one's abilities.

Social usage

The cultural phenomenon we call 'amateur photography' has been through a period of rapid change during the second half of this century. As the growth of Western economies has enabled new social groups access to leisure markets, these markets have changed.

Amateur photography has largely thrown off the formality of its first hundred years. Indeed, given the fact that such photography is the documentation of our social selves, it would be remarkable if it didn't reflect social change.

Pierre Bourdieu, writing in the 1960s,[20] saw vernacular photography as still essentially formal, a more or less 'official' record of rites of passage, especially weddings, anniversaries, comings of age and so on. It celebrated the unity of the family and served to integrate its members into that complex nexus of social relations. For Bourdieu, other amateur photography was associated with photographers or subjects who were not fully integrated into the family.

Boerdam and Martinius (1980) have since pointed to the historically and culturally specific nature of Bourdieu's data.[21] His analysis

More or less official records: The 'Passing Out' photo is typical of our 'integrative' pictures.

was based on information collected in rural France in the early sixties. By the late seventies this formal bias, predicated on the integrated family, was very much the exception rather than the rule. The modern world of individualism mitigates against regular expressions of wider solidarity.

Whilst Boerdam and Martinius do not see 'official' (probably professional) rite-of-passage photography being totally replaced, they do see another kind of photography as assuming prominence. This photography is a sort of 'talismanic' activity, it represents the 'best side' of the family/immediate social group, in a symbolic negation of the problems and stresses of living up to the happy family ideal. As the authors argue, 'From all kinds of events . . . people construct a "life in pictures" which can have great powers of conviction. It is a picture which is at once flattering . . . and "real" . . . By means of photographs people ensure for themselves a desired past in what would appear to be an objective manner.'[22]

Vernacular photography has changed since 1980, and is in a particular state of flux in the 1990s. With the relatively reduced costs, the amount of photography has mushroomed. We can afford to document more aspects of our social experience. What gets onto our film is diversifying all the time.

New subjects for our camera: As life brings us new experiences, sooner or later someone photographs them.

Instant access

Vernacular photographic activity is also changing under the influence of rapid technological change. Instant photography seems to have reached its peak in the mid-eighties. After Polaroid's successful prosecution of Kodak for patent infringements in 1984,[23] instant film prices have remained high relative to 35mm colour negative films and their prints. Their 'instant-ness' has been undermined by one-hour High Street processing. The instant feedback of a picture seconds after pressing the shutter doesn't seem to outweigh cost and availability differences. It is informative to consider why immediacy is not the overriding sales advantage many people thought it was in the 1970s.

To make use of the Polaroid's instant-ness, the photographer has to bring the instant print into the social situation. If done immediately this will usually change the atmosphere of the situation which claimed the photographer's attention in the first place. Instant reorganization of the event around the production of a print is unlikely to be experienced positively.

In the past, when normal prints took days or weeks to receive, instant photos offered the chance to re-create the event in a later situation, but still in the *special time* of 'holiday', 'Christmas', 'Wedding Fever' and so on. For instance, the prints of 'beach antics' could be re-circulated that evening as pre- or postprandial entertainment. Quick processing outlets in most holiday centres and large towns cater for such usage and so break instant photography's monopoly on this advantage.

Instant photography does allow the snapshooter to make sure of an acceptable result. But modern colour negative film and auto-exposure cameras ensure a high success rate too. Of course, video, that recent interloper into the vernacular mode, also allows for this instant check.

Video is being used instead of still photography to document the same events a camera would otherwise have been brought out for. Indeed, the 'palm size' camcorder is replacing the medium-priced SLR in the sales figures.[24]

But sitting in front of the telly watching hours of 'Bathing Baby', 'At The Seaside' or 'Christmas Party' is very different to flicking through stills, each of which is a whole story (*our version*) which can last for as little (or as much) time as we wish. Performing for video is also very different to being snapped. Sending a replayable video abroad is much harder than photos because of the incompatability of most national TV systems. So, it is harder for video to perform the old family integration role highlighted by Bourdieu for our modern dispersed families [see p. 55]. Finally, a video cassette is a poor substitute for the photo-memento. You can't carry it with you and steal a glance in your private moments. All in all, it doesn't seem that video will substantially take over vernacular photography's role.

Still video is in its infancy at the time of writing. Kodak is investing a quarter of a billion pounds to develop still video after the initial Japanese work brought it into our shops.[25] This suggests that it is set to become an influential photographic medium in the future. At the moment, as a medium for vernacular photography, it suffers from most of the problems I've outlined for videotape.

If still video can be arranged so as to produce paper prints of similar price, quality and availability to the current silver-based technologies, it could well take off. Instant viewfinder replay of the recorded image would allow the snapshooter to check quality, without feeling obliged to introduce the result into the situation. Easily available print-out facilities will fulfill the need for re-viewing in a social situation not dominated by the technology of replay. Viewing the snaps on TV is a problem because it dominates the social event in a way that passing prints around does not. (The book size portable video may change this.)

Video and still video can be expected to become an integrated package, so that photographers can choose which medium to use for whichever subject takes their eye. At the moment, the quality of video stills (as distinct from still video) is not sufficient to provide acceptable paper prints. However, these technologies may yet gain an economic edge as silver becomes scarcer. Silver is the precious metal upon which most photochemistry is based. Recovery of silver in the large D+P houses has slowed down the increase in rate of consumption. Now that the photographic market is becoming more sensitive to the problem of pollution, and because photochemistry is currently a high profile process compared to video image chip production, Green consumerism may well have its effect. Even so, it is an open question which is more environmentally damaging.[26]

Electronic storage of images may become a factor soon. As the dispersal of families continues, and different generations' multiple claims to ownership of images make copying whole albums desirable, an ability to do this simply may be favoured. Storage space is also becoming a problem. As snapshooting has mushroomed, so has the space our pictures take up.

The 'Photo CD' promises to be the sort of technology which can answer this problem. Currently, a cheap photo album can contain more images than such a compact disc, but it is bulky, whilst the CD can carry quite a number for its size. The agreement of international standards would enable dispersed families to keep in touch using this electronic format. If the price can be kept at least as low as an audio CD, then its compatibility with audio CD could lay the foundations for consumer interest.

5 Snap happy

Whilst some of us diligently put our photos in albums and regularly go through them with family and friends, most of us put them (still in their processing envelopes) in drawers and shoeboxes. After the initial flurry of interest, they are very seldom seen.

Given the photographs' relationships to our personal and social experience, it would seem a pity that we don't get more out of them. This chapter suggests some ideas in that direction. Hopefully, these may encourage some of us to value the enjoyment available in 'snaps' even more. These sorts of photos are not inferior to 'serious' photographs, rather they serve different purposes.

The act of taking a photograph marks an experience and values it. This personal statement can add to the meaningfulness of our lives. Sharing the experience can bring people closer and cement relationships.

One simple way to get 'added value' from photos is to send them as postcards. The pleasure of photography can be increased simply by an awareness of more people with whom we can communicate through our photographs. Making photos which we hope will be meaningful for them, as well as our regular audience, will make that small flush of creative excitement more frequent; as we think, 'This one's for X.' and, 'I must send a copy of this one to Y.'

Many of us brought up under the 'Protestant work ethic' feel a degree of guilt about using up a resource (film) on our own fleeting pleasure. This is dissipated somewhat by the simple act of regularly sending photos as postcards; also, it gets over the problem of keeping in touch when you've nothing to say, a reference to the image will suffice.

You can also turn the photos into cartoons by putting speech bubbles on to them. Peel-off labels are marketed especially for this usage [see p. 98]. Of course, these all-purpose stickers are shallow and we can heighten the fun of sending and receiving such 'autographs' by writing more personalized, self-reflexive bubbles on blank labels.

One of the things that writing on your photographs enables you to do is anchor their meaning [see p. 82]. This need not be a simple caption, but can have a more complex relationship (like the Leica caption to the 'young lovers' advert [p. 79]. It is surprising how much, and how soon, we forget about the circumstances of a photograph. But the techniques listed here can bring them back. Over the

'Let me stick one on you': Photo stickers available at chemists.

decades, this will enhance the evocativeness of snaps and provide a remarkable document and visual diary.

An interesting approach to photographs we have taken ourselves is to look for the personal symbolism they contain. Ralph Hattersley[1] has explored this area. He begins with the assumption that, 'Every photograph is a self-portrait'. In other words our preoccupations are displayed by our photos. It is a rare portrait that can do this with anything except superficial conviction.

Hattersley suggests that we look at our photos for themes and that we should be alive to such questions as: 'Is there a preponderance of a particular tone, colour or subject matter?', 'Why do I habitually take such shots?', 'What, if any, personal inner meaning do such preoccupations indicate?'. The analysis of the family album in chapter two may have given us some food for thought

Personal symbolism: The unmistakable signs of a Romantic, one of the author's snaps.

in this connection.

Our visual relationship to that depicted may be telling, too. If we regularly reproduce objects as distant, or close, does this signify any deeper personal attitude? A complete lack of such regularities may also be significant.

Asking such questions can open up a whole new area of self-

The author (Aged 15 months).

awareness. This in turn can produce fascinating contextualizing information for the photographs. Writing on the back of the photo keeps this sort of information relatively private when they are mounted in albums. A more public caption can be presented alongside the image. In years to come the differences (or similarities) may be particularly evocative.

Using audio tapes to contextualize photos is particularly appreciated by friends and relatives with whom you are not in regular contact.

Another way of extracting the contextualizing comments is to decode the photo for its absences and presences in a manner similar to that already practised on the AP images.

Photoanalysis

Robert Akeret in his remarkable book *Photoanalysis*[2] gives his approach to analysing family album photographs. He uses them to seek: '. . . exactly the same kind of information that we would be [seeking] if we were trying to make psychological observations from personal contact.'[3] Drawing heavily on theories of body language, he sets out a step-by-step process as a guide.[4] [A 20-step model is included as appendix one.] This has been adapted to serve as a model for our purposes. If we are alive to the possibilities of this sort of analysis, we will find ourselves intuitively following chains of questions, like some sort of 'photo-detective'.

The following analysis of a photo of the author as a toddler [p. 99] is the result of following in Akeret's footsteps. The relevance of each of his 20 questions varies from photo to photo, so I will not follow him rigidly. However, the model in the appendix should lead to success with most images. I have chosen an old image, rather than a current one, because it fits in with work described later in the chapter, but the approach's applicability to current images is, I think, clear.

Akeret recommended that we read a photograph like a page of text, from left to right and from top to bottom. This seems unnecessary for such an uncomplicated image as this. Straight away I can see that this is an unposed photo of me as a child in a garden. If I were to give it a title, it might be something like 'Come Down Here And Say That!'. An adult has taken the picture; judging by the high angle and the fact that, at the time, the only people in my family allowed to risk the expenditure of exposing film were adults.

It is interesting that for years until I really studied this photo, I had read the child's pose (my pose) as shaking his fist, now I can see that I am offering a long blade of grass to whoever is behind the camera. What I thought was a gesture of defiance, I now recognize

Censoring our past: We may remove people who are not to be spoken of from our albums, even to the extent of carefully cutting them out.

as one of friendship, even love.

I'm alone in the picture (not counting the photographer); my two older sisters are not there. This reminds me of how I was often not part of their games. As a younger brother, I was sometimes exactly the person they needed to exclude. Until looking at my family's snaps of us as children, I'd never realized this.

At the age depicted here, I was the typical healthy, chubby baby. Noting this recalls two things to mind. My sisters contracted polio, probably a year before this must have been taken. Careful nursing and state-of-the-art medicine pulled them through, but my parents had expected them to die. I didn't catch the disease, but gave my parents anxious moments by having the symptoms at the same time as my sisters (in fact I had a bad cold). As working-class parents, mine could not afford specialist health care, which must have increased their anxiety. Luckily, the family were visiting friends in a district which was served by the foremost polio team. This was in a National Health Hospital, which provided care free at the point of consumption. This health service had only been introduced by the post-war Labour Government during the previous decade. And so by being in the right place at the right time, my parents still have their family.

At this point in the photo-detective work, I would want to look for photos of my sisters and parents, before and after their ordeal. (It is very unlikely for there to be any taken during it. I would hope to empathize with their suffering, and joy at recovery.)

The other thing noticeable about how I look in this image is my chubbiness. At the time this was generally accepted in my mother's circles as being a good sign. 'Eat it all up, then you can have your pudding.' At the same time as food was used as pacifier and eating treated as an essential task, youth fashion was moving towards the worship of leanness. The conflicting signals surrounding food, often felt most strongly by mothers, certainly left their effects on my mother and me. To this day we both struggle with diets and being overweight. Although other photos show a well-proportioned 8–12 year old, until I reviewed these recently I did not have any recollection that I'd ever been of average weight. Hopefully this will be a new resource in my fight against flab.

It is important to remember that the sort of analysis recited above is not necessarily 'the truth'. It is 'a truth' which is productive now. The difference can be especially marked when (as is the case above) many years have passed since the image was taken. When the images are our own, and we've recently been involved in taking or posing for the image, we can arbitrate between possible readings. We have the other knowledge necessary to contextualize questions about relationships thrown up by Akeret's style of analysis.

With some of the thoughts brought out by 'photoanalysis' written on the back of the photo, looking at the image years later can prove a fascinating experience as we judge our comments with the addition of hindsight.

Photobiography

Since the 1970s, there has been an increasing concern in the West with our individual lineages. This may be related to the atomization of society, fuelled by geographical and social mobility and the socio-economic stress on the individual.

Whatever its cause, more and more people investigate their family trees and return to their childhood experience in an effort to discover how they got to be who they are. Investigating our family album can be a powerful source of understanding ourselves.

To start on this journey of discovery, collect together as many family photos from your near relatives as possible. Try to get people identified and the photographs dated. As you look through the photos, notice the recurrent poses and how similar some relatives look across generations. Connect family stories up to faces and put yourselves in their shoes. Look at the different ways people have changed with age. Look for pointed absences which your knowledge of family lore alerts you to. Who is not visible? What aspects of yourself and others are not depicted, and why?

After this preparatory groundclearing work, you are ready to try some of your own analysis on your own photos. Start with you at your youngest and move towards the present. Use Akeret's techniques [see appendix one] and the other decoding techniques from chapter three. Bear in mind that you are not necessarily finding out the material truth of your past through this process, but your own psychological truths now. They may be informed by your understandings of real events, and they may seem to be underpinned by the apparent objectivity of photography, but still they are essentially your truths, and that is where their value lies.

As you go through this process you may wish you knew more about how those close to you came to do what they did, and how they really felt. Use the photos of them, going backwards from the point at which they became an issue for you. Try to understand them, using the same techniques as you used on your own images.

This process can be vaguely interesting, or deeply moving, depending on our personal history and where we are in our own development. We can come to see the various ways we have been positioned, made visible (or invisible) and begin to have frames of reference for understanding our contradictory, many-faceted personality.

Since the early days of photography, many theoretically diverse approaches in the human sciences have used photography in their programmes.[5] The sort of approach discussed here is used as a diagnostic stage in various branches of counselling and psychotherapy. Here the general usage of photography tends to fit into three overlapping categories. Firstly, the photographic media are used to 'objectify' experiences (utilizing the power of photography's apparent realism). An example might be showing anorexics their own photo in a programme exploring body image and diet.[6]

Secondly, discussion of photographs is used to bring out thoughts and experiences that are problems for clients, and to use this, together with the objectification provided by photos for cathartic effect. For example, a client is encouraged to discuss ambiguous images. The generally-accepted referentiality of photographs is a useful asset in this instance.[7]

Thirdly, learning the skills of photography is used as a framework for building self confidence and a controlled introduction to social interaction. For example, disruptive school truants are put through a special course in photography.[8] (Often uses 1, 2 and 3 are combined in the course.)

In America, during the late seventies, these approaches began to be collected together and taught as a 'toolkit' for therapists of many different approaches. The champions of these techniques began to be known as 'phototherapists'.

'Photo therapy'

A process which has recently enjoyed publicity in Europe is an interesting amalgam of these. Simply known as 'photo therapy', its best known exponents are Jo Spence and Rosy Martin.

These two British women have developed their approach independently of the American 'phototherapists' and other more institutionalized approaches. For them it arises out of a need to create opportunities for making long-lasting personal, social, economic and political changes.

Both have visual arts and psychotherapeutic experience and training. Their involvement in photo therapy started with a concern to

Auto-phototherapy: The author gets back in touch with his youth through re-enacting a childhood snap (p. 99). The results show various gestures as he attempted to explore the possible emotions surrounding the initial image.

use photography to help ask questions (instead of apparently supplying answers), and to look for images which made connections to wider cultural codes. They wanted to ask questions about the contradictory nature of experience, and how this remains as tensions in our personalities. And perhaps most importantly, they were concerned to respond to the challenge of recognizing women's deep personal experiences as a basis for lasting political change. They had worked together for many months, building up a co-operative therapeutic relationship in Co-Counselling.[9] It is this basis of mutual trust and a shared approach which underpins all of their work. However, it may be possible for any of us to derive some benefit from exploring their approach on our own, with the support, but not involvement, of others. What must be remembered is that, for maximum effect and 'safety', a deeply trusting and accepting relationship of equal partners is necessary.

Without it, much of the power of the technique is lost, because unaided we cannot bring ourselves to confront our innermost contradictions in a sufficiently sustained manner. The growth of Co-Counselling and other vernacular therapeutic approaches means that it is possible for many of us to get the necessary support if we want it, but it does take time to build up the relationship.

It is possible to describe the stages of Spence and Martin's process, although again, it is only a guide to something which must be carried through as it 'feels right'. [Appendix two has hints on some technical aspects of the process.]

If you are going to experiment on your own, their first stage, building up the co-operative relationship, is replaced by the personal exploration process outlined so far [see pp. 100–103]. The second stage is to choose a photo which has particular connotations and raises questions/emotions which you want to explore. If you have decided to give the process a try, then you've probably already got one or more pictures which fit the bill.

Stage three is the process of actually photographing ourselves. In this stage we act out characteristics that have arisen from the photo as personally significant. Repeating poses, changing them for what was repressed, what *couldn't* be shown at the time. If possible, it is productive to act out those 'other selves' who never appear in photos, who were too sad, disruptive, shy or embarassed. Other roles can be explored and acted out, and what it feels like to inhabit their persona presented to the camera. One also explores how they might have acted if they'd allowed themselves to. All the time, as new poses and facial expressions emerge from the exploration, a self-portrait is taken.

It is not just the pose which is enacted, but small actions, characteristic expressions, 'nervous tics' – anything that can get close to the 'bare bones' of the subject. Some rudimentary costume and props may be necessary, especially if one is to act out characters of another gender.

This is the stage that most benefits from a co-worker – they can give encouragement and make suggestions. However, anything less than total trust and co-responsibility will hinder the process, rather than facilitate it.

When working in pairs, stage four is a post-session discussion. When experimenting alone, it may be a good idea to make a note of what thoughts and feelings arose in the session, and what poses provoked most reaction; including giggling, boredom, physical aches and pains, even yawning and shivering. It may well be that working on these poses in another session will produce further useful insight into one's personality.

The fifth stage occurs when the prints come back from the processor. (It is not a good idea to process your own images in this procedure.) Lay out the prints so that you can see all the images and look at the session as a whole. Use your notes from stage four to help pick out images and groups of images for further analysis. These can be decoded in the manner familiar from stage one.

This is another process that can be very emotional for people who've really got in touch with aspects of themselves and their loved ones which are normally hidden. As Jo Spence says one of her best sessions: 'When the prints arrived back through the post I cried for about an hour.'[10] The depth and power of her response is unlikely to happen to anyone without the help of an experienced counsellor/therapist. (For Jo this is a very *positive* expression of personal growth.) For others, however, the results may be equally revealing.

The final (?) stage is to take the knowledge gained from the whole experience and reassess it. This may well provide new insights which can be combined with other images to provide new starting points for the process to begin at stage three again.

At the centre of this therapeutic approach is the use of photography's powerful apparent objectivity. When the photos come back, *there you are* as you've not seen yourself before. Allied to this is the important fact that photographs have this 'realism', whilst always being open to being re-read. On their own, they are never contextualized enough. Split-second slices of time leave a lot of interpretation to be done. Frozen body positions, spatial relationships, facial expressions can all be read as instants from competing scenarios. We, the readers of the image, fill this information in.

I believe that most of us do not have special ways of thinking to bring to bear on photographs. We use those that we find applicable to the situation depicted, that is all we have. This is where the 'reality effect' of photography comes from. Psychologically, we use substantially the same process to interpret the photographically represented situation as we would the real situation. So in an important sense, they feel the same.

Because still photographs never anchor their meanings enough, (and indeed, all experience is open to reinterpretation) the meanings we invent for them are largely the products of our psychology. But at the same time, they derive their realism from the similarity of the way we have mentally processed them, and the way we process interpretations of the real. In this way photographs can objectify our inner world by a process of 'blanket authority' given by the 'reality effect' to our interpretations.

For this reason video is a different sort of therapeutic tool. Its apparent 'reality' is greater because movement and sound tend to erase the gap by which we become aware, however dimly, that we are going beyond what is given. Also, the continuous flow of time contextualizes any action, posture or expression. So, there is not much room for us to smuggle personally telling meanings under the 'blanket of authority'. Before we can ask ourselves whether or not that hand is raised in anger, decide it is, and then see its owner as 'really' ('reality effect') angry; his hat has been raised and this action followed by a smile.

The enhanced reality effect means that video is very good for witnessing how we appear to others. But it is not so good for projective work because it leaves less room for the play of personal meaning. It is a good starter in the area of confidence building through skills – as is instant photography – but it isn't as rich in potential, because the technology limits our involvement much more so than black-and-white photography.

Spence and Martin's approach has been called a process of 'self documentation' by Spence;[11] and Judy Weiser, a Canadian photo-therapist, has aptly described the whole genre as 'becoming visually literate about oneself'. She has also named the sort of approach I am outlining in this chapter as 'photobiography'.[12] These terms are to be preferred because they lose the connotations of 'therapy', which is assumed to benefit only the ill – those in need of 'fixing'. I believe that this process can be instructive and rewarding to anyone who has the time and the money to look at and take a few photos.

Using vernacular photography in the ways set out here can strikingly illustrate how the structures of society, its invisible norms and assumptions, can deeply effect our 'private' selves. The institutions we have to negotiate during our lives, family, school, church, government, even the armed forces, leave their marks, which can be traced in our albums.

Due to its intimate connection to one's life experience as documented by vernacular photographs, photobiography is a powerful personal tool for self assessment and change. In as much as personal change is a necessary corollary to social change, (which is in itself inevitable – the question is rather how to direct and divert change), photobiography can be a contribution to that change. In this scenario, vernacular photographs take on further social importance.

APPENDIX ONE

Akeret's procedure can be summarized as 20 steps which can be laid out as follows:

1 What do we immediately see in the photo? (Try giving it an evocative title).

2 What is obviously happening? Is there anything more subtle going on?

3 Is the photo candid or posed? (How much control did the photographer exercise and who was it?)

4 Is the background significant? (Really, or symbolically).

5 What feelings does the photo evoke in you?

6 What physical intimacy or distance do you notice? Are people touching, and if so, how?

7 How do the subjects feel about their bodies? Do they show them off, hide behind them, use them seductively?

8 What emotional state do people appear to have? (Akeret gives a list including 'compliant, mad, sexy, lonely, . . .' and many others which would seem to potentially tell us more about our current selves than about the subject of the photograph.)

9 Try to see how these emotions are expressed by facial dynamics and body movements, e.g. are they relaxed or tense? (This may act as a check upon the worst excesses of the analyst's fantasies, encouraged by step 8.)

10 What is noticeable about the various parts of each person? Start with the general body posture and then move out to hands, arms and legs. Then pay particular attention to the face, eyes and mouth. Are the parts in harmony, or contradiction?

11 Is there more than one person (including animals) in the image? If so, what is the group mood? How do they relate to each other? Who has the power? Where is the love? Who protects whom?

Going over the photograph repeatedly, looking for the subtle as well as the obvious, ask some more general questions.

12 What pointedly does not appear? i.e., what would be called into question if the image were otherwise?

13 What is the cultural background/social class of those depicted? If it is a family photo, and not your own, would you like to be a

member of the family, would you let your children play with theirs?

14 Is the activity associated with one particular gender? – by the people depicted? by society then? by society now?

15 What memories and experiences does the photo stir in you?

16 Do you identify with the people in the photo? How are you alike and how unlike them?

17 What is most moving in the photo? Does it disturb you? Is it distasteful?

18 If the photo features you, how have you changed since then? How are you the same?

19 Is there a sense of movement, and if so, where is it? If the photo came alive what would happen? Project yourself into the situation, how would you feel?

20 Is the photo one of a series? If so, use the series to contextualize each shot and help anchor the meaning of frozen actions. Look for themes running through a series and then look for their meaning.

Akeret's approach has been criticized over its assumption that what is being elicited from the photographs are properties of the images and those depicted in them, rather than the projections of the analyst. In his defense, he regularly cautions us against reading too much into the image and stresses the importance of other information to help fix the multiple meanings of such images. If we are our own image analysts, then as long as we remember that what emerges from the procedure is our own truth, these reservations with the Akeret technique are not important.

APPENDIX TWO

Photobiography

Resources:

To carry out a self-documentation session, certain easily available equipment and facilities are necessary:

1 A reasonably empty room, if possible 3.5 metres or more long. Try to choose one with a bare wall at one end; this provides the background.
2 A camera with flash. The cheapest suitable camera is a compact with built-in flash. If it can be afforded, one with autowind is best. Second-hand compacts are often a good bet. Any camera of higher specification is suitable as long as it can be linked to an electronic flash. Completely automatic cameras can be fooled by a light wall – use the backlight facility if it has one.
3 A tripod or support. Compact cameras are light enough to be taped to broom handles and the broom stuck in the back of a chair, for example. The elegance of the support is not at issue.
4 A long (4–6 metre) air shutter release cable. Most compacts do not have a method of attaching such units to the camera, so here is a method of overcoming the problem: take the circular cap from a plastic film canister and make a hole in the middle, slightly smaller than the screw thread of the air release. Then screw the thread of the release into the top of the cap so that it is firmly attached. This can now be taped over the shutter release button such that it is only operated by the air release.
5 A film. The cheapest film on offer is acceptable for this work. 100 ASA colour films from supermarkets are fine.

If you don't already have any of the above, starting from scratch may cost £25 ($35) or more. After that the cost of film, processing and flash batteries are the only outlays.

Procedure:

Make sure you have an hour or two when you'll be uninterrupted. Usually the camera should be set up vertically to allow for full-length pictures. This also results in a camera-subject distance something like the best focus position for simple lenses.

Don't forget to load the film carefully and to check its passage through the camera before fixing it into position and attaching the air release.

Make sure that the settings are correct for the film, flash and distance. Use fresh batteries each session.

Clear the background of any unnecessary detail, such as wallhangings.

Set up your props, change clothes or whatever you need to do to create the effect.

Place the air release bulb on the floor so that it can be operated by your foot.

Using the original photo as a reference, try to start getting into the 'mood' and begin to try out poses, facial expressions etc. As each change feels achieved, or particularly difficult, take a photo as and when you feel like it. Obviously an autowind greatly facilitates this procedure. Don't forget to allow time for the flash to recharge (ten seconds should be enough). At the end of the session take the batteries out and use them for something else. There is nothing worse than ruining a session because the flash did not work reliably.

In this work it is advisable to use a postal development and printing service. This is because the anonymity of the system adds to your feeling of security in the session. Also, it is important that the images come back to you after a delay and from an impersonal source. This enables a lot of psychological 'distance' to be created between you and the photos. When finally confronted with the results of the session, some will bridge this gap and strike you the more forcibly for their apparent objectivity.

Instant photographs can be powerful tools for remodelling poses, but they tend to pull our concentration out from our internal states and into self-conscious questions of appearance which are perhaps best left till later. For a similar reason I would not recommend a mirror in the session, except as a prop. In the end, of course, it is up to the individual.

GOOD LUCK!

NOTES AND REFERENCES

INTRODUCTION
1. R. Williams, *Keywords (A Vocabulary of Culture And Society)*, Fontana, 1976.

CHAPTER ONE
1. There are many claimants for the title 'inventor of photography'. Experiments came to fruition in France and England around the same time. Daguerre's process produced one-off images which could not be reproduced. See: H. Gernsheim, *The Origins Of Photography*, Thames and Hudson, 1982.
2. This is based upon a yearly wage of £40 and Beard's monthly takings of over £800. Of course his profit would not be so extensive. However, it is difficult to be accurate about the yearly wage figure. Hobsbawm says that half of the manual labour class made only £25 to £30 in 1867, and wages were lower in the forties. See Gernsheim, ibid, p. 127. E.J. Hobsbawm, *Industry And Empire*, Penguin, 1969, pp. 154–62.
3. The histories and interrelationship of patents and copyright is a complex subject. Basically France and England, the two centres of photographic invention, had different histories. England's patent law was confused until 1852 and many of photography's early gentlemen inventors were at the forefront of pushing for clarification. France had been one of the first nations to create a patent statute which removed the question of state patronage and upheld a right of inventors to profit from their invention. In the area of copyright too; England and France took different approaches. France looked to provide the maximum protection to the author of a creative work, England wished to protect the author enough to encourage production and dissemination, but no more. These fundamental differences must be borne in mind when dealing with the mass of legal wranglings which resulted from photography in its early years. See Edleman's work on French copyright developments and Buckland's comments on Fox Talbot's patent problems. G. Buckland, *Fox Talbot And The Invention Of Photography*, Scolar Press, 1980, (cf. pp. 35–7 and 104–14). B. Edelman, *Ownership Of The Image; Elements For A Marxist Theory of Law*, Routledge and Kegan Paul, 1979.
4. Photography was invented during the height of Chartism and general unrest of the labouring classes. Working hours were extreme and it took 35 years to reduce the working week of regulated workshops to $56\frac{1}{2}$ hours. Holidays, vastly reduced by the

new labour system of industrial production were not reintroduced until the last quarter of the century. Best (79) estimates that 'Periods of holiday with pay seem to have been virtually unknown among wage earning manual workers before the 1880s.' (op. cit. p. 226). Workers had to struggle for these advances, they were not won easily, See: G. Best, *Mid Victorian Britain*, Fontana, 1979 (cf. pp. 120–40 and 218–36).

5. Hobsbawm, ibid. pp. 157 and 168.

6. J. Stevenson, *British Society 1914–1945*, Penguin, 1984, pp. 39–44 and 117–141.

7. It is all too easy to forget that, despite the large drop in the cost of photography instigated by Eastman and his Kodaks, even the 25p Brownie was an expense beyond the thoughts of most people. I feel that manufacturer's claims to the contrary must be taken with a pinch of salt (see p. 73, note 4). An appraisal better than most but still inclined to over stress the devolution of photography to all social groups is presented by Ford. See: C. Ford, *The Story Of Popular Photography*, Century Hutchinson Ltd/ NMPFT, 1989, pp. 62–9.

8. For the sorts of people who clubbed together to buy family cameras (the labouring classes), wages were about £2.50 per week for men. A film with eight pictures cost something over an hour's wages (6p) and processing and printing it cost another 9p, or more than an hour and a half's wages. The most common film length nowadays is 24 frames, so our shooting power per film would have cost almost a day's wages for families between the wars.

9. The average industrial wage in the thirties was £3.00 per week in Britain. As is still the case today such averages are higher than the most usual wage. The price for a Leica is taken from adverts in the *Amateur Photographer* of 1936.

10. See article on worker photography in *Photography/Politics One*,

11. Two books which deal with these approaches in Britain are widely available, the second also mentions the worker photography of the 30s. S. Bezencenet and P. Corrigan, *Photographic Practices: Towards A Different Image*, Comedia Publishing Group, 1986. S. Braden, *Committing Photography*, Pluto Press, 1983.

12. M. Vicinus, *A Widening Sphere: Changing Roles Of Victorian Women*, Methuen, 1980, cf. pp. XVI–XIX.

13. Hobsbawm, ibid. p. 168.
A discussion of the legacy of this state of affairs is contained in the article listed below:
L. Bland, 'Guardians of The Race, or Vampires on The Nation's Health? Female Sexuality and its Regulation in Early Twentieth Century Britain', in E. Whitelegg et al, *The Changing Experience Of Women*, Martin Robertson/Open University, 1982.

14. I would argue that this is an understatement. For a discussion of some of the effects this sort of photography may have, see: R.

Coward, *Female Desire: Women's Sexuality Today*, Paladin 1984, pp. 19–82 and 99–106.

15. For two conflicting versions of this pivotal dispute for British politics, see:
L. Levidow, 'Grunwick: The Social Contract Meets The 20th Century Sweatshop', in Levidow, L. and Young, B., *Science Technology and the Labour Process: Marxist Studies Volume 1*, CSE Books, 1981, pp. 123–71. G. Ward. *Fort Grunwick*, Maurice Temple Smith Ltd., 1977.

16. H. Gernsheim, *Julia Margaret Cameron: Her Life and Photographic Works*, Gordon Frazer, 1975.

17. D.A. Kenyon, 'Snap Judgements; Towards a Phenomenology of The Vernacular Photographic Act', Unpublished dissertation, Department of Film and Media Studies, University Of Stirling, 1989, pp. 97–100.

18. Good examples of this approach are those articles written under the influence of the French philosopher/historian Michel Foucault. In photography, the most influential exponent is probably John Tagg. His book contains several of his long historical essays.
J. Tagg, *The Burden Of Representation*, Macmillan, 1988.

CHAPTER TWO

1. This list is taken from the information displayed in the 'current photography' section of the Kodak Museum at the National Museum of Photography, Film and Television (NMPFT). This has been combined with another such list compiled as part of my own research, reported in my unpublished M. Litt. dissertation, [op. cit.].

2. NMPFT, ibid.

3. Kenyon, ibid. pp. 111–14.

4. Kenyon, ibid. pp. 115–19.

5. Kenyon, ibid. pp. 120, 122 and 128–30.

6. Kenyon, ibid. pp. 132–3, 141 and 171.

7. Kenyon, ibid. pp. 101–4.

8. This seems to be a fairly frequent occurrence. See M. Lieberman, *Art Therapy for Groups*, Croom Helm, 1986, p. 49. Also, G.A. Kelly, in: B. Maher, (ed.) *Clinical Psychology and Personality: The Selected Papers Of George Kelly*, John Wiley and Sons Inc., 1969, pp. 253–6.

9. P. Pacey, *Family Art*, Polity Press/Basil Blackwell, 1989, p. 79.

10. A detailed discussion of the development and current state of women's ideological connection to nature and motherhood can be found in the Open University's Course 221. See 'The Changing Experience Of Women', L. Birke, *Unit 3, Nature and Culture: Women as Part of Nature*, Open University Press, 1983, pp. 15–17. Also, R. O'Day, *Unit 7, Women in the Household: A Historical Analysis 1500–1850*, Open University Press, 1983, pp. 20–28.

11. Again this is discussed provocatively and in depth in the Open

University Course 'The Changing Experience of Women'. See, D. Leonard, and M.A. Speakman, *Unit 9, The Family: Daughters, Wives and Mothers*, Open University Press, 1983.

12. Kenyon, ibid. pp. 99–100.
13. J. Berger, *Ways of Seeing*, BBC and Penguin, 1972, 1985 ed., pp. 106–8.
14. *Amateur Photographer*, May 23, 1987, p. 6 and April 9, 1988, p. 6.
15. The journal *Leisure Studies* has contained many reviews of the field with good references. Some are listed below:
    A. Colley, 'Sex Roles And Explanations Of Leisure Behaviour', *Vol 3/3*. Sept' 1984, pp. 335–41.
    R. Ingham, 'Psychological Contributions to the Study of Leisure – Part One', *Vol 5/3*, Sept 1986, pp. 255–79.
    N.C.A. Parry, 'Sociological Contributions to the Study of Leisure', *Vol 2/1*, Jan 1983, pp. 57–81.
    R.W. Vickerman, 'The Contribution of economics to the Study Of Leisure', *Vol 2/3*, Sept 1983, pp. 345–64.
    B. Wearing, and S. Wearing, 'All In A Day's Leisure: Gender and the Concept of Leisure', *Vol 7/2*, May 1988, pp. 111–23.
    J. Zuzanek, and R. Mannell, 'Work-Leisure Relationships from a Social and Social Psychological Perspective', *Vol 2/3*. Sept 1983, pp. 327–44.
16. Kenyon, ibid. pp. 99–100.
17. Kenyon, ibid. pp. 100 and 103–4.
18. *Amateur Photographer*, 13 October, 1990, p. 7.
19. Jo Spence, the photographer and author of several articles and a book *Putting Myself In The Picture* has told me in conversation that when researching in a large processing laboratory she found that the employees expected a certain amount of this material as 'normal' for a day's through put. This is confirmed by Graham King in his book. See; G. King, *Say 'Cheese': The Snapshot as Art And Social History*, Collins, 1986, p. 47.
20. The question of 'The Look' has been approached from the standpoint of a reading of Freud by Laura Mulvey, most notably in an article published in 1975. Halla Beloff has criticized this approach in her book *Camera Culture*. In general, cultural studies have too readily accepted psychoanalysis as the only suitable paradigm for understanding the construction of people as subjects. It is only recently that theory has begun to draw upon other approaches with which to open some of the limitations of psychoanalysis. See:
    H. Beloff, *Camera Culture*, Basil Blackwell, 1985, pp. 67–73.
    J. Henriques, W. Hollaway et al, *Changing the Subject: Psychology, Social Regulation and Subjectivity*, Methuen, 1984. cf. section 3 'Theorizing Subjectivity', pp. 203–322.
    L. Mulvey, 'Visual Pleasure in Narrative Cinema' in *Screen* 16/3, 1975, pp. 6–18.

21. O'Day, ibid. pp. 33–44. (See note 10.)
22. R. Barthes, *Camera Lucida*, Fontana/Flamingo, 1984, pp. 11–15.
23. Beloff, ibid. pp. 185–7.
24. This is a scenario which was described to me by one of the respondents in my research project. When repeated to other respondents, it seemed familiar to many of them. Jeremy Seabrook has linked the tradition of women as domestic narrators with the social function of vernacular photography to record our social relationships. In the article listed below he questions whether this role will survive our period of rampant individualism and reduced social networks.
    J. Seabrook, 'My Life is in the Box', *Ten. 8* 34, Autumn 1989, pp. 34–41.
25. J. Boerdam, and W.O. Martinius, 'Family Photographs – A Sociological Approach' in *The Netherlands Journal Of Sociology* 16/2, 1980, pp. 95–119.
26. Fox Talbot, the inventor of the negative/positive process took just such a photograph in Rouen in 1843.
    G. Buckland, *Fox Talbot And The Invention of Photography*, Scolar Press, 1980, pp. 74&75.
27. D. Maccannel, *The Tourist: A New Theory of The Leisure Class*, Schocken Books, 1976, pp. 105–7.
28. A. Tomlinson, and H. Walker, 'Holidays for all: Popular Movements, Collective Leisure, and the Pleasure Industry' in A. Tomlinson, (ed.) *Consumption, Identity, and Style*, Comedia, 1990, pp. 221–41.
29. M. Cerullo, and P. Ewen, 'Having A Good Time; The American Family Goes Camping', in *Radical America* 16/1 and 2, 1982, pp. 13–43.
30. Maccannel, op. cit.
31. Boerdam and Martinius, op. cit.
32. P. Bourdieu, et al. *Un Art Moyen (Essais Sur les Usages Sociaux de la Photographie)*, Les Editions de Minuit, 1965, Chapter One, pp. 31–106. Translated by S. Whiteside and published as *Photography: A Middle Brow Art*, Polity Press, 1990.
33. Pacey, ibid. pp. 65–9.
34. J. Ruby, 'Portraying the Dead' in *Omega* 19/1, 1988/9, pp. 1–20, cf. p. 5.
35. R. Williams, *The Country and the City*, Chatto and Windus, 1973. This book looks at the development of our modern notions of the country and city through consideration of literature from Classical Greece to the recent past. From this base, Williams throws light on many issues concerning the land and our attitudes to it. See also: J. Taylor, 'The Imaginary Landscape', *Ten 8* Vol 12, Winter 1983, pp. 2–13. In this article Taylor looks at the favoured image of the countryside since photography's invention.
36. In Britain's multi-racial society, immigrants are concentrated in

towns and cities. They visit the countryside much less frequently than the average. Some claim that this is due to feeling unwelcome in rural communities. This would suggest that parks may feature more prominently as signs of landscape for these groups. It is just these sorts of difference in the inflection of subject matter and treatment, based as it is upon differential social experience that gives the term *vernacular* its descriptive power when applied to amateur photography.

37. Photo-pictorialism was certainly not unchallenged during the period. More modern visual approaches were championed by many of the photographic artists still revered by the popular photo press (revered, one suspects, mainly for being famous). At the time, established amateurs (as represented by *The Amateur Photographer*, for instance) actively fought these new approaches and claimed pictorialism as the aesthetic true to photography. See:
J. Taylor, 'Pictorial Photography in Britain 1900–1920', in Barry Lane, (ed.) *Pictorial Photography In Britain 1900–1920*, Arts Council of Great Britain, 1978, pp. 9–32, cf. pp. 13–22.
T. Morden, 'The Pastoral and the Pictorial', *Ten. 8* 12, Winter 1983, pp. 18–25.

38. This was a thread uniting the consideration of nineteenth-century philosophy, literature and art of the Open University's Arts Foundation Course A101. The text most closely associated with the considerations of this book are contained in units 22 and 23 which draw particularly on the work of Klingender. See:
S. Bayley, *Units 22&23, Nature, Work, And Art*, The Open University Press, 1978, cf. pp. 5–16.
F.D. Klingender, *Art and the Industrial Revolution*, Evelyn, Adams and Mackay, 1968.

39. N. Bryson, *Vision And Painting: The Logic Of The Gaze*, Macmillan, 1983, pp. 104–8.

40. G. Porter, 'Trade And Industry' in *Ten 8* 35, Winter 1990, pp. 45–48, cf. p. 48.

41. This observation, initially made by animal behaviourists, has become part of the general knowledge of photographers. Walt Disney exploited this in his characterization of a young deer in the shape of 'Bambi'. Exaggerating these traits of the human infant has spawned a whole popular illustrative style for greetings cards and the like. For it's application to our idea of 'cute' baby photos, see:
G. Izzi, *Photographing People*, Century Hutchinson Ltd, 1987, p. 214.

42. *Amateur Photographer*, 23 May, 1987, p. 6 and 9 April, 1988, p. 6.

43. *Amateur Photographer*, 1 September, 1990, p. 6 and 7 July, 1990, p. 7.

CHAPTER THREE

1. *Popular Photography*, Diamandis Communications Inc., 1633 Broadway, New York, USA.

2. *Petersen's PHOTOgraphic*, Petersen Publishing Co., Sunset

Boulevard, Los Angeles, California, USA.

3. This format of article continued throughout the 1930s. It was placed just before the art pages and referred to at least one reproduction there. It aimed to impart knowledge of photographic skills from a successful exhibitor to the general readership.

4. Colin Ford in his *The Story of Popular Photography* draws attention to the increased proportion of female and working class male camera users occasioned by the introduction of cheap roll film cameras prior to the First World War. Whilst I do not doubt that the percentages increased, I doubt that they really reached the proportions claimed by the photographic trade of the time. A certain amount of hyperbole can, I think, be assumed. When an industry wishes to widen its market, it often tells the new target group that its members are already consumers. It cannot be doubted that women have been used extensively in photographic advertising since the Edwardian period, but this usage is much more complex than simply constituting an appeal to women. See:
C. Ford, *The Story of Popular Photography*, Century Hutchinson with NMPFT, 1989, pp. 37, 38 and 65–9.

5. John Berger in *Ways of Seeing*, (Penguin, 1972, Chapters 3 and 5) asserts that oil painting is particularly involved with vicarious possession, or celebration of actual possession, even of the nude. I agree with his argument, but think in this case it is a matter of degree. In the thirties there were much less circumspect images available, and today the nude is not treated in such a classical manner in the amateur press. Now nudes are an occasion for celebration of their sexuality, not an opportunity to test the subtlety of the materials and techniques.

6. R. Barthes, 'Myth Today', in *Mythologies*, Paladin, 1973, pp. 109–59.

7. E. Goffman, *Gender Advertisements*, Macmillan Press Ltd., 1979, pp. 28 and 43.

8. Personal interview with George Hughes, 19 October 1990.

9. By the beginning of 1991 the editorial policy on covers had changed. In a reply to a letter printed on the 12 January edition the editor writes '. . . there have been quite a few non-glamour covers of late. [. . .] On the covers of those [using women] . . . the models were not always scantily-clad. In short, AP is making an effort to introduce a wider range of subjects to its cover. We will continue with this policy if you continue to buy the magazine! Rival magazines on the other hand, still persist with a semi-naked-woman approach.'

10. The American work seems to underestimate the reasons that people join any sort of club. Things like 'getting out of the house' – meeting new people similar to oneself etc. My experience suggests that photography is pretty much a pretext for a social gathering of like-minded people. Sometimes it could almost be an alcohol appreciation society or a sports club. The American research seems

to have alighted on fairly old fashioned clubs. Modern technology and advertising have changed the assumptions and demands of many amateurs that attend clubs. The prevalence of courses at evening class, and in further education means that the aspiring photographer has plenty of alternatives to the camera club if they are just keen to know more. The links of class to geographic area and therefore to the sort of club that may result have not been investigated either. Bourdieu's work in France in the 1960s should alert us to possible connections. See:

P. Bourdieu, (ed,), *Un Art Moyen (Essai Sur Les Usages Sociaux de la Photographie)*, Les Editions de Minuit, Paris 1965. (See Part 2, Chapter 1 pp. 144–172.)

R.W. Christopherson, 'From Folk Art To Fine Art: A Transformation in the Meaning Of Photographic Work', *Urban Life And Culture*, 3/2, July 1974, pp. 123–157. (This is interesting for its parallels with the Schwartz article, even though it describes artists who see themselves as distinct from camera clubbers.)

D. Schwartz, 'Camera Clubs and Fine Art Photography (The Social Construction of an Elite Code)', *Urban Life* 15/2, July 1986, pp. 165–95.

CHAPTER FOUR

1. This information comes from the following sources:
    The estimate of the number of photographs in the nineties, *Signals*, British television programme for Channel Four, Autumn 1989.
    America's volume in 1974 is from G, Freund, *Photography And Society*, Gordon Fraser, 1980, p. 203.
    The 1987 UK expenditure on photography is from the text of the National Museum of Photography, Film and Television, Bradford, Yorkshire, (NMPFT).
    The information on Japan comes from *Amateur Photographer*, 16 September, 1989, p. 7.

2. The comparison with wrist watches comes from the TV programme *Signals* too.
    The percentages of people over 15 and of households having more than one camera come from my: 'Snap Judgements: Towards a Phenomenology of the Vernacular Photographic Act', Unpublished M. Litt. dissertation, University of Stirling, 1989, pp. 93–9.

3. G. Porter, 'Trade and Industry', *Ten 8* no. 35 Winter 1990, pp. 45–8 (page 47).

4. *Amateur Photographer*, 7 July, 1990, p. 7.

5. Evidence of manufacturers' 'greening' comes from the news pages of *Amateur Photographer*, cf. 18 November, 1989, p. 11, and *Amateur Photographer*, 29 January, 1990, p. 11.

6. Porter, ibid., p. 48.

7. In my research [op. cit.] women still reported less interest in photography than men, despite continued targeting from the advertisers. Although women under 35 would seem as likely as men

to take photos, they are less likely to spend a lot on photography. Society's general divorcing of women from technology, can only add to women's alienation from an activity so heavily marketed on techno-fetishism. Indeed, marketing aimed at women is almost exclusively intended to get them to join the ranks of 'non committed' photographers [see pp. 89–90]. Many women already occupy this position. Further involvement and the increased expenditure which goes with it, remains unlikely when all the marketing ploys for this sector are aimed at men.

8. *Amateur Photography*, 7 July, 1990, p. 7. Also, 1 September, 1990, p. 6.
9. D. Slater, 'Marketing Mass Photography' in Davis, H. and Walton, P., *Language, Image, Media*, Blackwell, 1983, pp. 245–63, (page 253).
10. Slater, ibid.
11. Nowadays in Britain, the developing and printing is controlled by less than ten independent business men. What effect this will have on the market is yet to be seen. [ref. *Amateur Photographer*, 18 August, 1990, p. 13.
12. For Slater, this well known slogan encapsulates one of the main problems with mass photography: control of the creative process is removed from the picture taker.
13. *Amateur Photographer*, 14 October, 1989, p. 13.
14. Porter, ibid., p. 48.
15. Slater, ibid., p. 254.
16. Porter, ibid., p. 46.
17. Porter, ibid.
18. Slater, ibid., p. 255.
19. G. Eastman, 'Letter to M.G. Peck, January 19th, 1892' quoted in Newhall, B., *The History Of Photography*, Secker and Warburg, 1972, p. 94.
20. P. Bourdieu, et al., *Un Art Moyen (Essais Sur Les Usages Sociaux De La Photographie)*, Editions de Minuit, 1965.
21. P. Boerdam, and W.D. Martinius, 'Family Photographs – A Sociological Approach', *The Netherlands Journal Of Sociology*, vol. 16/2, pp. 95–119 (pages 96–99).
22. Boerdam and Martinius, ibid., p. 116.
23. *Amateur Photographer*, 28 September, 1985, p. 7. After a nine year battle, the American courts finally ruled that Kodak had infringed seven of Polaroid's patents. Kodak were prohibited from making or selling instant cameras. Still it took a further five years for the courts to agree compensation to Polaroid ($910 million) in October 1990. In July 1991, Kodak finally paid $925 million. (*Amateur Photographer* 27 July 1991, p. 8.)
24. *Amateur Photographer*, 1 September, 1990, p. 5.
25. *Amateur Photographer*, 11 August, 1990, p. 7.
26. In 1988 it emerged that Kodak had allowed the leakage of thousands of gallons of potentially carcinogenic solvents into a

populated area of Rochester NY (Kodak's H.Q.). This created bad publicity and undermined its generally good relations with the city it helped to build up. This occurred just at the time that photographic manufacturers began to use environmental concerns as a marketing gambit. The production of many hi-tech components involved in the manufacture of other recording media require the use and storage, of agents even more deadly (with the concomitant risk of accidental release into the environment.) The final product alone is not a suitable indicator of its pollution potential. The whole process of its manufacture, distribution and disposal, needs to be investigated for its environmental impact. See:

L.U. Marks, 'Kodak's Latent Image: Toxic Spills in the Company Town', *Ten. 8* 34, Autumn 1989, pp. 10–19.

For a fascinating account of the company-resident-media-triangle which developed over a year of local action. See T. Bennett et al., *Culture, Ideology And Social Process*, Batsford, 1981.

CHAPTER FIVE

1. R. Hattersley, *Discover Your Self Through Photography*, Morgan and Morgan Inc., 1976.
2. R.U. Akeret, *Photoanalysis*, Simon and Schuster, 1973.
3. Akeret, ibid., p. 33.
4. Akeret, ibid., pp. 33–46
5. There have been countless programmes using photography since its early days. Anthropology, social work, sociology, criminology, medicine, psychology and many more disciplines have used photography. The sources listed below are merely a beginning.
M. Banta and C.M. Hinsley, *From Site to Sight: Anthropology and the Power Of Imagery*, Peabody Musuem Press, 1986.
J. Collier, *Visual Anthropology: Photography as a Research Method*, Holt, Rinehart and Winston, 1967.
E.J. Janis and W. Macneil (eds), *Photography Within the Humanities*, Addison House, 1977.
D.A. Krauss and J.L. Fryrear (eds), *Photography in Mental Health*, Charles C. Thomas Publishers, Springfield, Illinois, 1983.
R. McGrath, 'Medical Police' *Ten 8*, 14, Summer 1984, pp. 13–18.
J. Tagg, 'Power and Photography – A Means Of Surveillance: The Photograph As Evidence In Law', in: T. Bennett et al., *Cultural Ideology And Social Process*, Batsford, 1981.
J. Wagner, (ed), *Images Of Information: Still Photography In Social Science*, Sage, 1979.
6. A. Byrne,. 'Photography for Anorexia Nervosa' *British Journal Of Psychiatry*, No. 153. 1988, p. 848.
Also: B.E. Williams, 'Reaching Adolescents Through Portraiture Photography', *Child And Youth Care Quarterly*, 16/4, 1987, pp. 241–8.
7. J. Walker, 'The Use of Ambiguous Artistic Images for Enhancing Self-Awareness in Psychotherapy', *The Arts in Psychotherapy*, No.

13, 1986, pp. 241–8.

8. C. Cosden and D. Reynolds, 'Photography as Therapy', *The Arts In Psychotherapy*, No. 9, 1982, pp. 19–23.

9. Co-Counselling is practised by an international network of like-minded individuals. It is based on the theories of Harvey Jackins. An introduction is:
    H. Jackins, *The Human Side Of Human Beings*, Rational Island Publishers, Seattle, 1st pub. 1965, 16th edn. 1985.

10. R. Martin and J. Spence, 'New Portraits for Old: The Use of The Camera in Therapy', *Feminist Review* No. 19, 1985, pp. 67–92, (page 91).

11. J. Spence, 'Disrupting the Silence: The Daughter's Story', *Oral History*, Spring 1990, pp. 54–60 (page 56).

12. J. Weisser, 'Phototherapy – Becoming Visually Literate About Oneself' *Phototherapy* Vol 4, No. 2, pp. 2–7 (page 4).

FURTHER READING

BARTHES, ROLAND, *Image – Music – Text*, Fontana, 1977.
 Several of the essays collected in this volume are relevant. The first three on photographic images are most obviously apt. 'Introduction to The Structural Analysis of Narratives' and 'Change The Object Itself' are also related. The latter is a continuation of Barthes's deliberations in 'Myth Today'.
DEWDNEY, ANDREW and LISTER, MARTIN, *Youth, Culture And Photography*, Macmillan Education Ltd., 1988.
 This is a great source book for those setting up projects with a critical approach to photography. The authors draw on their copious experience of this sort of work to both discuss the issues surrounding youth and photography, and to describe projects which tackled these issues.
GREENHILL, RICHARD, MURRAY, MAGGIE, and SPENCE, JO, *Photography*, Macdonald Guidelines Series, Macdonald Educational Ltd., 1977.
 This inexpensive book gives most of the basic information about photographic principles and techniques that the amateur photographic press trades on. It very definitely does not link this to copious photo-consumption. It also contextualises photography within the wider issues of society's use of representations in general. As a basic photography handbook this has not been surpassed.
HARDYMENT, CHRISTINA, *From Mangle to Microwave: The Mechanisation of Household Work*, Polity Press, 1988.
 This book looks at some of the consumer items which competed with cameras for the family's expenditure. She shows that such equipment could have developed very differently and that technology, economics and politics interact to form our everyday domestic environment.
HIRSCH, JULIA, *Family Photographs: Content, Meaning And Effect*, Oxford University Press, 1981.
 One of the few intelligent books on the subject. Hirsch relates photography to other modes of representation, in its usage as a family documentation medium.
HOLLAND, PATRICIA and SPENCE, JO (eds.), *Family Snaps: The Meanings of Domestic Photography*, Virago 1991.
 This volume collects 30 articles, most not published elsewhere. They address many issues ranging from photography and our sense of self to the political potential of amateur photographic documents. A must for those concerned in taking the issues raised here further.
MEDIA EDUCATION, (c/o Tower Arts Centre, Romsey Rd, Winchester, Hampshire, SO22 9PW).
 This magazine is aimed at the teacher working outside of Higher Education. It is full of useful and provocative articles based upon teachers' own experience of running projects.
MOCS (Magazine Of Cultural Studies), (c/o 15 Gateacre Rd, Woolton, Liverpool, L25 5NL).
 This is a new magazine, published by a collective of people involved in cultural studies and working in Higher Education. It aims to present readable and provocative material on general cultural issues. Photography features occasionally, but its main assets are its accessibility and relevance as background information to the more specialized texts.
MUSELLO, CHRISTOPHER, 'Family Photography' in WAGNER, JON, *Images Of Information*, Sage Publications Inc., 1979.
 This American article was ground breaking in its vernacular focus and its

treatment of photography as a social event. It has been influential in recent thinking about the sociology of vernacular photography.

NICHOLS, BILL, *Ideology And The Image*, Indiana University Press, 1981.
This book contains, in its introduction and first two chapters, one of the most readable and sensible primers for the sort of image analysis practised here.

SPENCE, JO, *Putting Myself In The Picture*, Camden Press, 1986.
This is an autobiography. It documents the author's experience of using and thinking about photography over 35 years. Spence has been involved in some of Britain's most groundbreaking radical photographic ventures. Much of her work since 1982 has been concerned with health, especially cancer, and the relationship between patients and the medical establishment. Together with Rosy Martin she has developed and publicized a particular version of Photo Therapy in Britain.

SUDJIC, DEYAN, *Cult Objects*, Paladin, 1985.
A light hearted look at the meanings of products as diverse as gumboots and cigarettes. Sudjic maps out modern 'taste' with entertaining glee. Pages 58–65 touch briefly on cult cameras, the Leica, Minox, Polaroid SX70, and perhaps surprisingly, the Olympus XA.

TEN.8.
This magazine is the only one currently published in Britain that is dedicated to photography, and its critical appraisal as a cultural act. It regularly publishes articles similar in their approach to this book's. It also publishes good reproductions of fine photographs by photographers who elsewhere receive less recognition than they deserve.

WILLIAMS, VAL, *Women Photographers: The Other Observers, 1900 To The Present*, Virago, 1986.
This concentrates on British women and is a timely reminder that despite wider forces, not all successful photographers have been men.

WILLIAMSON, JUDITH, *Decoding Advertisements: Ideology And Meaning In Advertising*, Marion Boyars, 1978.
This is still *the* reference book for this sort of image analysis. The advertising industry has read it and learnt its lesson well. The final chapter is perhaps the most prophetic for the development of advertising images since the book's publication.

WINSHIP, JANICE, *Inside Women's Magazines*, Pandora, 1987.
This book is a nice compliment to the detailed analysis of texts and images such as Williamson's. Winship still manages to retain a 'normal reader's' interest, even after her 20 years of critical engagement with magazines. The book contains histories of the market and individual titles, together with analyses of adverts, covers and articles. It lays particular stress on decoding typical content in order to illustrate ideology at work.

INDEX

Note: Page references in *italics* refer to illustrations and captions.